Activating Assessment for All Students

Other Titles of Interest by Mary Hamm and Dennis Adams

Tomorrow's Innovators: Essential Skills for a Changing World
Demystify Math, Science, and Technology: Creativity, Innovation, and Problem-Solving
Helping Students Who Struggle with Math and Science: A Collaborative Approach for Elementary and Middle Schools
Shaping the Future with Math, Science, and Technology: Solutions and Lesson Plans to Prepare Tomorrow's Innovators

Activating Assessment for All Students

Differentiated Instruction and Informative Methods in Math and Science

Second Edition

Mary Hamm and Dennis Adams

ROWMAN & LITTLEFIELD EDUCATION
A division of
ROWMAN & LITTLEFIELD PUBLISHERS, INC.
Lanham • New York • Toronto • Plymouth, UK

Published by Rowman & Littlefield Education
A division of Rowman & Littlefield Publishers, Inc.
A wholly owned subsidiary of The Rowman & Littlefield Publishing Group, Inc.
4501 Forbes Boulevard, Suite 200, Lanham, Maryland 20706
www.rowman.com

10 Thornbury Road, Plymouth PL6 7PP, United Kingdom

Copyright © 2013 by Mary Hamm and Dennis Adams

All rights reserved. No part of this book may be reproduced in any form or by any electronic or mechanical means, including information storage and retrieval systems, without written permission from the publisher, except by a reviewer who may quote passages in a review.

British Library Cataloguing in Publication Information Available

Library of Congress Cataloging-in-Publication Data Is Available

ISBN 978-1-4758-0198-9 (pbk. : alk. paper)
ISBN 978-1-4758-0199-6 (electronic)

Contents

1. Instructional Assessment: Formative Assessment, Differentiation, and Science/Math Examples ... 1
2. Integrated Performance Assessments: Informative Methods for Assessing Differentiated Learning ... 23
3. Science Instruction: Inquiry, Teamwork, and *In*formative Assessment ... 43
4. Mathematics Instruction: Differentiation, Problem Solving, and Formative Assessment ... 65
5. Lesson Plans for Science and Math: *In*formative Assessment and Adjusting the Teaching/Learning Process ... 91

ONE

Instructional Assessment

Formative Assessment, Differentiation, and Science/ Math Examples

> *As the brain has a tendency to organize and seek patterns, so does the human being organize the world, internal and external, into meaning. We must remain vulnerable to that world—even while taking an evaluative and critical stance.* —Robert Kegan

Just about everyone seems to agree that an important predictor of student success involves having a well-qualified teacher. Of course, deciding who can put the best instructional and assessment techniques to good use is just as hard as finding really good teaching candidates and keeping them on the job.

Checking for understanding and providing students with constructive feedback are part of every successful teacher's tool kit. Constructing authentic assessment tasks that connect to realistic settings is one of the characteristics of effective instruction. The same can be said for gathering information based on performance to facilitate student achievement.

This chapter examines formative assessment practices and uses science and math examples to explore multiple entry points to knowledge. It also

- examines the principles that guide differentiated learning.
- suggests classroom activities that build on multiple intelligence theory.
- assists teachers in lesson planning and using adaptive teaching strategies.
- introduces ways for teachers and students to do their work collaboratively.

- makes suggestions for performance assessment and portfolios.

Modern assessment techniques are designed to help teachers figure out where they are going and how well students are moving in that direction. The basic idea is to understand what's happening today and to look forward in a way that will help solve future problems.

Although the focus here is on formative assessment and differentiation, we occasionally use the term *instructional assessment* to cover a wider range of informational assessments that can be used by teachers and students.

Although most teachers have curriculum guidelines to follow, they can still teach in ways that make the material meaningful and understandable. Also, teachers usually have enough space for decision making to differentiate and use formative assessment in ways that ensure their students' academic success.

ASSESSMENT AND QUALITY INSTRUCTION ARE INSEPARABLE

Although standardized testing is beyond the scope of this book, it is important to note that student achievement tests only supply useful hints about learning and teaching effectiveness. They are not designed to identify who is a good teacher and who isn't. Also, the tests are so narrow that teaching to the test would result in a warped educational process.

Recent research on teacher effectiveness suggests that standards-based evaluation is often associated with student learning gains. Also, National Board certification and performance assessments for beginning teachers include evidence of student work as well as effective teaching practices (Darling-Hammond et al., 2012).

We do know that the successful teachers provide their students with frequent (ongoing) feedback about their work. There is also general agreement that all teachers improve instruction by adapting and differentiating instruction based on a wide range of *in*formative assessments (Popham, 2011).

Exploring what students understand as they go about their work is now considered essential to good planning and high-quality instruction. So it is little wonder that teachers are more interested than ever in learning about *formative assessment* (Clarke, 2008).

High-quality assessment methods and effective instruction are as inseparable as teacher improvement and professional development. It is hoped that the assessment ideas and techniques presented here will help. They all involve collecting information about students and making decisions about *what* to teach and *how* to teach it.

Formative assessment often takes place *during instruction*—allowing teachers to quickly provide feedback and make adjustments that will help ensure students' success. Clearly, instruction can be improved by doing a better job of understanding how learning is progressing. Self, peer, and teacher understanding are all part of the process. The basic idea is to help everyone understand what knowledge and skills are emerging—along with valuing alternate time frames and different depths (Bailey & Jakicic, 2012).

A formative assessment system is a powerful way to enhance student achievement. Formative assessment establishes a purpose for each lesson, alerting students to important information which promotes feedback and allows the teacher to check for understanding.

Various forms of instructional assessment can be used to establish a need for differentiation. If teachers know where students need to be—and consistently check to see where they are—differentiation can be an effective way of helping students succeed (Wylie et al., 2012).

INSTRUCTIONAL ASSESSMENT AND THE DIFFERENTIATED CLASSROOM

Although teachers may be receptive to differentiation and formative assessment, many are not fully prepared to implement these techniques in their classroom. When you were in elementary school, teachers knew that they were supposed to give tests and grades but probably had little understanding of the role of ongoing assessment in a dynamic and success-oriented classroom. We've learned a lot since then.

The following are important points about modern classroom assessment:

1. *Assessment is much more than testing*. Students explore many ways to show their understanding of what they know. Some students do badly on tests but show other evidence of learning. They solve problems, are involved in class discussions, contribute important ideas, draw sketches, and may role-play when they want to communicate. There are many ways that students can express their learning. When given multiple ways to show their understanding of what they know, more students are engaged.

Authentic student accomplishments come alive as we watch students learn. One form of assessment doesn't work for everyone. When things don't work out, it may indicate a poor match between the student and the method used by the teacher to find out what the student knows.

It is important not to settle for a single assessment strategy (such as testing) as an adequate representation of what students understand. It's necessary to look beyond testing to discover just what students understand.

2. *Differentiated instructive assessment is not about grades*. When teachers try to figure out what individual students know, understand, and can do, it becomes much more interesting than assessing by judging students for

their accomplishments. Rather than ranking students, the teacher's role shifts to guiding students toward success. Teachers quickly discover that giving students feedback about their work is more productive than giving grades. They become more respectful of the students and their possibilities. Teaching for success and focusing on students' accomplishments plays a crucial role in instructive assessment.

3. *Differentiated instructional assessment is informal.* When you see how students work collaboratively with others or choose to work alone, you can get a sense of their disengagement or misunderstandings. Often, you find out information by just watching student behavior or reading the students' journals.

Assessment can occur at any time, whether you are searching for it or not. Talking to students in purposeful ways as you observe their actions is an informal way of assessing. It is helpful to take notes about your students as you focus and move around the room. Virtually all students can provide valuable assessment tools when you look for individual strengths and accomplishments.

4. *Differentiated instructional assessment is part of curriculum planning.* When teachers begin to understand the importance of planning, they know precisely what matters most for students to understand and to be able to do. Creating lesson plans and designing units are essential in good teaching. Teachers come to realize that assessment often originates from what happens *during* the teaching process.

Learning goals that match students' needs when linked with differentiated instructional assessment are a major part of curriculum design. Feedback is not enough. Formative assessment establishes a purpose with basic objectives. It guides instruction using good questions, promoting collaborative group work. The key is individual accountability—the instructor goes over students' work products to determine which students need additional attention (Frey & Fisher, 2011).

5. *Differentiated instructional assessment is an ongoing process.* Rather than administering an assessment at the end of a unit, instructional assessment that occurs during the unit is very involving. Teachers use instructional assessment to help them become better teachers. It is important to lay out precisely what matters most for students to learn and to be able to do. When the teacher studies students' work during the course of a unit, he or she can do many things to support the student who is, or is not, falling behind. Students who are not grasping the content may need further explanations or demonstrations offered in a different way. Teachers need to know when to reteach or when to move ahead.

6. *Differentiated assessment can be part of quality instruction.* Knowing what students care about and how they learn provides options for students to show what they understand. When teachers tap into students' strengths and give them something to build on, they spend time gather-

ing assessment information on what students can do. This helps teachers recognize that all students have strengths from which all can benefit.

7. *Differentiated assessment requires a partnership in student success.* Differentiated instructional assessment is for students and teachers. As students become better learners, they understand the learning objectives, know what success is, and understand how each assignment contributes to their success. They develop a sense of self-efficacy—a feeling of internal control that causes them to work harder (Tomlinson & McTighe, 2006).

We need to examine the differences among *assessment about learning* (judging students' performance), *assessment for learning* (sparking better teaching), and *assessment as learning* (where knowledge is communicated to the teacher and the student). When ongoing assessment is viewed as an important part of student learning, it becomes a catalyst for better teaching (Webber & Lupart, 2012).

LOOKING AT DIFFERENTIATED INSTRUCTIONAL ASSESSMENT TOOLS

Teachers carefully plan in order to reach every student. Many try to differentiate, becoming aware of the opportunity to reach the distinct needs of the classroom population. Many teachers also use differentiated tools that help organize and alter instruction in a way that provides the best learning opportunities for each student. Accomplishing this task requires rules and routines that are carefully selected to meet learners' changing needs.

Today, educators are using several differentiated instruction activities or techniques to adapt the ideas and change the old way of doing things. Some of the modern approaches that teachers now use include

- providing a comfortable and stimulating learning environment.
- evaluating students' individual needs before, during, and after instruction.
- using evaluation data to carefully plan interesting lessons.
- selecting and organizing activities for classes, individuals, partnerships, and small groups.
- encouraging each student to continue to learn and improve.

TEACHERS' DECISIONS AND OPINIONS ARE CRUCIAL

A teacher's view when evaluating students' data is very important. For example, when the students' data are analyzed, the teacher makes a judgment on how to use the results. The standard and the content information are chosen to reach each student. Selection, organization, and pacing of instruction for each student are determined by the student's knowledge base, cultural background, strengths, needs, interests, and learning styles.

Each teacher has an individual management style that is mirrored in his or her daily teaching. "Knowing your students" becomes a critical part of differentiated instruction. Differentiated instruction, in turn, puts students at the center of learning and allows their learning needs to help teachers manage instructional planning. The first step in differentiated learning is to begin where you are.

Differentiation does not mean throwing out your planning methods from past years. It means analyzing how well you're providing variety and challenge in learning, recognizing which students are best served by your current plans, and altering those plans as needed so that more students can be successful.

DIFFERENTIATED LEARNING GOALS

We know knowledge continues to expand as we gain more information about how the brain learns. Our views about effective teaching and learning are based on the latest brain research that informs our work. Following are some of the goals of effective differentiating learning. Teachers should

- involve students in activities that respond to their individual needs, strengths, and inclinations.
- develop challenging and engaging tasks for every learner.
- present management strategies to include flexible grouping approaches to content and instruction.
- pay attention to students' readiness, instructional needs, and learning preferences.
- aid in the process of gathering and organizing assessment data.

We encourage readers to choose and adapt these ideas and suggestions as they arrange their classrooms for differentiated instruction and assessment.

ORGANIZING FOR INSTRUCTIVE DIFFERENTIATED INSTRUCTION

Differentiated learning involves orchestrating instruction to provide each student with many positive, nourishing, and successful learning experiences. The plan is to meet the learning requirements of students with a wide range of needs and academic abilities.

Differentiated instruction (DI) involves recognizing the fact that individuals and small groups of students can use different content, processes, and results to achieve the same conceptual understanding. Instructional differentiated responses from the teacher can be as simple as rephrasing a question—or as complicated as regrouping on the basis of student needs and interests.

DI is different from individualized learning or designing a lesson for every student. It involves building mixed-ability group instruction around the idea that individual students (or groups of students) learn in unique ways and at varying levels of difficulty. Observation and assessment can lead along a similar path.

A good way for learning groups to connect with differentiated instruction is for teachers to base group assignments on what they know about the interests and aptitudes of the students involved. There are times when students may need multiple chances to demonstrate mastery. In a differentiated classroom, you will find students doing more thinking for themselves *and* working more with peers.

Self-evaluation and a gentle kind of peer assessment are part of the process. With differentiated instruction, small collaborative groups within the class are often working at different levels of complexity and at different rates. Science and math lessons can be differentiated based on a student's interest in these subjects, readiness to learn a concept, and preferred path to comprehension.

Differentiated instruction is most effective when science/math concepts are taught in context and related to relevant prior knowledge. DI can provide multiple paths to understanding and expressing what has been learned. The process involves having learners construct meaning by working with peers to explore issues, problems, and solutions. In this way, differentiated instruction is different from individualized instruction in that it moves beyond the specific needs and skills of each student to address the needs of clusters of students.

MULTIPLE PATHS TO LEARNING AND ASSESSMENT

Differentiated instruction is not a totally new concept for teaching elementary and middle-school students. Teachers have always been faced with the challenge of dealing with the fact that individual students learn things in different ways. Yet tracking didn't seem to do anybody much good. Differentiated learning involves building mixed-ability group instruction around the idea that individual students learn in unique ways and at varying levels of difficulty (Tomlinson, 2003).

DISCOVERING WAYS TO DIFFERENTIATE INSTRUCTION

In a differentiated classroom, the teacher accepts students as they are and helps them succeed by considering their unique circumstances. Differentiated classrooms are places where the teacher carefully designs instruction around the concepts, principles, and skills at the core of the subject being studied. The teacher makes sure that learners focus on essential understandings and important skills. Subjects are introduced in a way that all students are likely to find them meaningful and interesting.

Recognizing individual learning styles and adapting a differentiated teaching style can make learning easier. With differentiated learning, the teacher provides specific ways for each student to learn deeply, working energetically to ensure that all students work harder than they thought possible and achieve more than they imagined.

Learners in the same classroom have different backgrounds, strengths, needs, interests, and subject preferences. Some students learn subjects like science or math easily, while others struggle. The ones who have trouble in science and math may shine in language arts and social studies.

It is up to the teacher to create an active classroom environment that optimizes learning for students with quite different abilities and interests. In such a differentiated classroom, teachers purposely plan to meet each student's varied needs within a framework of established standards.

It helps if students know the purpose and the importance of each lesson. Fixed ideas about intelligence and excessive praise can be harmful. When purpose works with goals and students are motivated, formative assessment can enhance the learning process (Dweck, 2007).

SAMPLE STRATEGIES FOR HELPING TEACHERS DIFFERENTIATE INSTRUCTION

Student readiness involves current knowledge, understanding, and skill level. In a differentiated classroom, teachers provide books at different reading levels and use activities at various levels of difficulty that may focus on the same learning goal.

Interest is another factor differentiating instruction. Teachers often let students choose from a variety of media arrangements such as video, music, film, and computers to express their ideas. Students might, for example, write about their favorite movie or examine their thoughts about the music that excites them. Another possibility is illustrating topics of interest. Teachers can vary the activities based on the interests and the aptitudes in a way that allows everyone to reach the same concept, although they may go about it differently.

MULTIPLE ENTRY POINTS TO KNOWLEDGE

Today's classrooms are challenging environments for teachers. Designing lessons that are responsive to the individual needs of all students is not an easy task. Skills such as communicating, observing, reasoning, measuring, making connections, experimenting, and problem solving are only a few of the processes involved in doing science and math.

Teachers in differentiated classrooms begin with a clear understanding of what represents a powerful curriculum and engaging instruction. They then accommodate instruction so that each student comes away with deeper understandings and skills.

> *The biggest mistake of past centuries in teaching has been to treat all children as if they are variants of the same individual, and thus to feel justified in teaching them the same subjects in the same ways.* —Howard Gardner

Howard Gardner's framework for multiple entry points to knowledge has had a powerful influence on differentiated learning and the content standards. There are differences, but each set of standards is built on a belief in the uniqueness of each student and the view that this can be fused with a commitment to achieving worthwhile goals. Also, being able to base instruction on a student's preferred way of learning is especially helpful in reaching everybody in the classroom.

A TEACHER'S VIEW OF MULTIPLE INTELLIGENCES

1. Linguistic intelligence is the capacity to use language to express ideas, excite, convince, and convey information. This includes speaking, writing, and reading.
2. Logical-mathematical intelligence is the ability to explore patterns and relationships by manipulating objects or symbols in an orderly manner.
3. Musical-rhythmic intelligence is defined as the capacity to think in music, the ability to perform, compose, or enjoy a musical piece. Musical intelligence involves understanding rhythm, beat, tune, melody, and singing. Students can use musical instruments or make their own.
4. Spatial intelligence is the ability to understand and mentally manipulate a form or object in a visual or spatial display. This includes maps, drawings, and even electronic media.
5. Bodily-kinesthetic intelligence is the ability to use motor skills in sports, performing arts, or art productions (particularly dance or acting).
6. Interpersonal intelligence is something students use all the time. The ability to work in groups, interact, share, lead, follow, and reach out to others is part of interpersonal intelligence.
7. Intrapersonal intelligence is the ability to understand one's inner feelings, dreams, and ideas. Intrapersonal intelligence involves introspection, meditation, reflection, and self-assessment.

8. Naturalist intelligence has to do with observing, understanding, and organizing patterns in the natural environment. It is the ability to discriminate among living things (plants, animals) as well as to develop a sensitivity to the natural world.

WAYS TEACHERS CAN TEACH THE INTELLIGENCES

Here are some ways to spice up any regular lesson with each of the "intelligences." You don't have to try to use all of them for each lesson or attempt to master all the intelligences at once. Select a few of your favorite techniques in any of the intelligences or one teaching method from each intelligence and try to work them into your day.

Linguistic Intelligence

This intelligence has a natural carryover to science and math instruction. Linguistic intelligence has gotten a lot of focus in the science and math standards. According to the educational standards, the study of science and math should include many opportunities for communication so that students can

- reflect on and clarify their thinking about mathematical and scientific ideas and situations;
- realize that representing, discussing, reading, writing, and listening to science and mathematics are an important part of science and math learning;
- model situations using oral and written methods; and
- evaluate science and math ideas. (National Academy Press, 1996; National Council of Teachers of Mathematics, 2000)

Sample Linguistic Intelligence Techniques

After the student has found a pattern in his or her exploration, ask for a generalization of the pattern.

- Have students try to communicate the pattern they found by writing, in two complete sentences, what they observed. Have them describe the pattern in general terms.
- Encourage students to describe, step by step, what procedure they used to arrive at a solution.

Spatial Intelligence

Sample Spatial Intelligence Techniques

When explaining a science or math procedure, have students make a diagram that shows the procedures they used to get an answer.

- Have students make a flowchart that shows the steps they must do to complete the task (for example, measure the distance).
- Use manipulatives to model science and math concepts and skills.
- Encourage students to draw a picture or make a design of something they are trying to remember.

Musical-Rhythmic Intelligence

Sample Musical-Rhythmic Intelligence Techniques

- Play three to five minutes of classical music before starting to learn tasks.
- Use sound breaks between activities to energize waning energy and low moods.
- Use clapping, singing, humming, rhythmic movement, rhythmic words (raps), or jingles to help students recall and recite concepts. Example: Sing the fours multiplication table to "Jingle Bells" (starting with "Dashing through the snow"): "One times four is four, (and a) two times four is eight, three times four is twelve, four fours are sixteen, five fours are twenty," and so on.

Bodily-Kinesthetic Intelligence

Sample Bodily-Kinesthetic Intelligence Techniques

- A major kinesthetic tool is the use of manipulatives: Linking cubes and base-ten blocks can be used to model math concepts of place value and regrouping. Pattern blocks can be used to create spatial geometric learning.
- Science rock searches or leaf explorations use this intelligence. Students describe and gather natural objects.
- Play physical games to practice science and math concepts. Hopscotch or Twister designed for math facts practice works well. Card games and board games like Concentration or Scrabble redesigned for use with number cards and markers also works. Students can help with the design and rules of the game.

Interpersonal Intelligence

Sample Interpersonal Intelligence Techniques

- Use collaborative learning techniques often. They will enhance students' learning experiences.
- For example, students can work together to create a five-minute commercial about outer space, the moon, black holes, or faraway planets.
- Encourage students to play two- or three-person math and science games to practice basic skills (card games such as forehead poker or Go Fish can be used).

Logical-Mathematical Intelligence

Sample Logical-Mathematical Intelligence Techniques

- Encourage mental math daily. Whenever possible, request that students attempt to do the simpler calculations in their heads.
- Encourage estimation. "How much do you expect the answer to be? For example, for 24 × 18, think 25 × 20 = 500, which would serve as a good guess.'"
- Use natural objects to model math and science concepts and processes. Examples: Use petals, small rocks, and hard berries as counters to model sorting, counting, subtraction, place value, averaging, and so on.
- Use natural settings to teach math and science concepts. Example: "Estimate the number of needles on this evergreen tree. Back your estimate with counts and calculations that justify your guess."
- Use sorting and classifying as a way to make science and math terms comprehensible.

Within a multiple-intelligences (MI) framework, intelligence might be defined as the ability to solve problems, generate new problems, and do things that are valued within one's own culture. MI theory suggests that these eight "intelligences" work together in complex ways. Most people can develop an adequate level of competency in all of them. And there are many ways to be intelligent within each category.

Will the intelligences covered by multiple intelligence theory be as central to the twenty-first century as they were to the twentieth? It is possible to take issue with MI theory on points, like not fully addressing spiritual and artistic modes of thought. But there is general agreement on a central point: *Intelligence is not a single capacity that every human being possesses to a greater or lesser extent.*

No matter how you explain it, there are multiple paths to competency in basic subject matter. Also, it makes sense to use formative assessment techniques so that differentiated instruction can be effectively used in a way that builds on different ways of knowing and understanding (Keeley, 2008).

CONNECTING THE MIND, BRAIN, AND EDUCATION

A number of new ideas have come from psychology, cognitive science, and related research about how the brain functions. We now understand many things about teaching, learning, and how the mind works that we didn't know about even a few decades ago. For the past decade or so, researchers have been trying to understand the mind's capabilities and figure out how the results might be applied to learning.

Although connecting brain research to actual classroom practice remains a problem, the gap is being closed. Differentiated learning, for example, builds on some of the new ideas gleaned from cognitive science and brain research, and goes on to suggest using a balance of visual, auditory, oral, and written materials to match the preferences of different kinds of learners (Schank, 2011).

Research in brain physiology, genetics, and cognitive science has proliferated in recent years. Research on the mind and the brain involves a collaboration among biology, education, and the cognitive and developmental sciences. With the availability of so much new and promising information comes opportunities for teachers to gain new insights into human behavior and educational practice.

As research contributes more to usable educational knowledge, classroom practitioners can help to refine the promising possibilities. And they can add practical meaning to an environment where new ideas are welcomed and, at the same time, are critically examined.

As educators explore the intersection of mind, brain, and education, they will come across information that will have a positive impact on their teaching. For example, we now have some idea of how brain cells are malleable or plastic enough for learning to occur and how they remain stable enough for the learning to solidify into knowledge. Early childhood experiences matter, but those first three years are not quite as critical as was once thought.

There are findings in neuroscience that suggest it is not just a question of losing brain neurons as an individual ages; thousands of neurons are formed every day and migrate into areas of the brain in charge of intelligence, decision making, and problem solving.

An important message here is that the brain is an ever-changing place that is very responsive to experience. Our brains remain remarkably plastic and we retain the ability to learn throughout our lives (Jenson, 2005).

NEW DESIGNS FOR TEACHING AND LEARNING

Like cognitive science and its associates, the field of education is constantly growing and changing. We now have a better understanding of both the problems and the possibilities associated with teaching children and young adults. The science and math standards have helped by building on the research to inform practice.

Until well past the midpoint of the twentieth century, the theoretical ideas about learning were dominated by a behaviorist view of reward and punishment. Over the past few decades, the cognitive perspective has largely taken its place. Cognitive science suggests ways for thinking about how the mind works and how knowledge is acquired and represented in the memory system.

Developments in neuroscience have further extended the field of cognitive science. Brain research suggests not only that students learn best in different ways but also that collaborative group work can inspire their best efforts. However, this doesn't mean that students shouldn't pursue learning projects on their own or work with a partner.

Cognitive science, multiple-intelligence theory, differentiated learning, and constructivism are, at least, all indirectly related. Constructivist educators emphasize teaching students to classify, analyze, predict, create, and solve problems. Student ability to learn new ideas is viewed as having a lot to do with the information an individual has prior to instruction (Battro, Fischer, & Lena, 2007).

Facts can be important building blocks, but constructivist teachers emphasize actively building new structures on prior knowledge. In the differentiated classroom, carefully designed student-centered learning along with a self-reflective teaching can ensure that we are serving students of diverse abilities and interests. This goes beyond helping struggling students to making sure that all students perform as well as they can.

Opinions about the usefulness of brain research, cognitive science, and educational research may vary, but you can be certain that a more thorough understanding of the human brain will be an even more important part of our expanding educational knowledge base in the future.

Clearly, the differentiated instruction notion of helping each child succeed in numerous and varied ways will be part of the formula for keeping all students involved and successful. It is also clear that students from different cultural and economic backgrounds will need extra inspiration and multiple approaches for learning subject matter.

MULTIPLE ENTRY POINTS TO KNOWLEDGE

Learning has a lot to do with finding your own gifts. Many questions remain, but no one doubts that today's students are a complex lot, with varying needs, abilities, and interests. Making learning more accessible to such a wide range of students means respecting multiple ways of making meaning. The brain has a multiplicity of functions and voices that speak independently and distinctly for different individuals (Battista, 2012).

No two children are alike. An enriched environment for one is not necessarily enriched for another. The basic idea is to maximize each student's learning capacity. We use the term *differentiated instruction* (DI) to refer to a systematic approach to teaching academically diverse learners.

DI is a way of thinking about students' learning needs and enhancing each student's learning capacity. This approach suggests that teachers become aware of who their students are and how student differences relate to what is being taught. The hope is that by having the flexibility to differentiate or adapt student assignments, teachers can increase the possibility that each student will learn (Keene, 2012).

IMPORTANT PRINCIPLES OF DIFFERENTIATION

There are several key principles that describe a differentiated classroom. A few of them are defined here:

1. *An engaging quality curriculum* is the first fundamental principle. The teacher's job is to guarantee the curriculum is inviting, consistent, important, and thoughtful.
2. Students' work should be satisfying, inviting, stimulating, and thought provoking. *All students should find their work interesting and powerful.*
3. Teachers should attempt to *assign tasks that are a little too difficult* for the student. Be sure there is a team assigned to support or assist the students.
4. *Use flexible grouping.* It is important to plan times for groups of students to work together—and times for students to work independently. Provide teacher-choice and student-choice groups.
5. *Assessment is an ongoing process.* Preassessment bases students' knowledge and skills on students' needs. Then, teachers can differentiate instruction to match the needs of each student. At final assessment time, it's important to plan several assessment strategies, for example, using a quiz and a project.
6. *Grades should be based on growth.* A student who persists and doesn't see progress will likely become frustrated if grade-level benchmarks remain out of reach and growth doesn't seem to count. It is the teacher's job to support the student.

Over the past few decades, researchers have suggested that since the human brain is "wired" in different ways, it is important for teachers to realize that students learn and create in different ways. Although it is often best to teach to a student's strength, we know that providing young people with deep learning experiences in different domains can enrich their intelligence in specific areas (Bailey & Jakicic, 2012).

BUILDING ON DIFFERENT INTELLIGENCE PREFERENCES

Sternberg has contributed to the awareness that students exhibit different intelligence preferences. He suggests three intelligence preferences: analytic (schoolhouse intelligence), creative (imaginative intelligence), and practical (contextual, street-smart intelligence). Gardner originally suggested seven "intelligences" and went on to explore exemplary examples (Gardner, 1993). He continues to develop ways of understanding the multiplicity of intelligences and attributes that can be found in the classroom (Gardner, 2011).

Activities That Reflect Multiple Intelligence Theory

1. Upper-elementary and middle-school students can comprehend MI theory. Why not explain it to them and have them do some activities to remember it?
2. We like having students work with a partner.
3. Encourage various learning styles:

    Mastery style learner—concrete learner; step-by-step process; learns sequentially.
    Understanding style learner—focuses on ideas and abstractions; learns through a process of questioning.
    Self-expressive style learner—looks for images; uses feelings and emotions.
    Interpersonal style learner—focuses on the concrete; prefers to learn socially; judges learning in terms of its potential use in helping others.

4. Build on students' interests. When students do research either individually or with a group, allow them to choose a project that appeals to them. Students should also choose the best way for communicating their understanding of the topic. In this way, students discover more about their interests, concerns, learning styles, and intelligences.
5. Plan interesting lessons. There are many ways to plan interesting lessons.

Lesson Planning

1. Set the tone of the lesson. Focus student attention; relate the lesson to what students have done before. Stimulate interest.
2. Present the objectives and purpose of the lesson. What are students supposed to learn? Why is the lesson important?
3. Provide background information. What information is available? Resources such as books, journals, videos, pictures, maps, charts, teacher lectures, class discussions, or seat work should be listed.
4. Define procedures. What are students supposed to do? This includes examples and demonstrations as well as working directions.
5. Monitor students' understanding. During the lesson, the teacher should check students' understanding and adjust the lesson if necessary. Teachers should invite questions and allow students to ask for clarification. A continuous feedback process should be in place.
6. Provide guided practice experiences. Students should have a chance to use the new knowledge presented under direct teacher supervision.
7. It is equally important that students get opportunities for independent practice where they can use their new knowledge and skills.
8. Evaluating and assessing students' work is necessary to show that students have demonstrated an understanding of significant concepts.

A Sample Multiple Intelligence Lesson Plan

Differentiated Brain Lesson

The basic idea is to develop understandings of personal health, changes in environments, and local challenges in science and technology. The human body and the brain are fascinating areas of study. The brain, like the rest of the body, is composed of cells, but brain cells are different from other cells.

A Sample Lesson Plan

This lesson focuses on the math standards of problem solving, estimation, data analysis, logic, reasoning, communication, and math computations. The science standards of inquiry, life science, science and technology, and personal and social perspectives are included.

Lesson goals: The basic goal is to provide a dynamic experience with each of the eight "intelligences." Map out a chart on construction paper.

Procedures:

1. Divide the class into groups. Assign each group an intelligence.

2. Allow students time to prepare an activity that addresses their intelligence. Each small group will give a three-minute presentation (with a large map) to the entire class. Let reluctant students see, hear, touch, and write about new or difficult concepts. Utilize materials that assess present learner needs. Allow the class to develop its own problems

Grade level: With modifications, K–8.

Activity 1—Introduce graphic organizers   Graphic organizers help students retain semantic information. Mind mapping or webbing illustrates a main idea and supporting details. To make a mind map, write an idea or concept in the middle of a sheet of paper. Draw a circle around it. Then draw a line from the circle. Write a word or phrase to describe the idea or concept. Draw other lines coming from the circle in a similar manner. Then, have students draw pictures or symbols to represent their descriptions.

Multiple Intelligences Learning Activities

Linguistic: Write a reflection about the activity, and keep a study journal.

Evaluation: Each group will write a reflection on its activity. Journal reflections should tell what the students learned about neurons and how that helps them understand how the brain works. Encourage students to organize their work and put it in a portfolio.

If either you or your students want to find or publish information about math or science topics, such as the human brain (or anything else), we suggest trying Digital Universe (digitaluniverse.net). It combines some of the wide-reaching strengths of Wikipedia with the trustworthiness of Britannica. Anyone can contribute to the Digital Universe online encyclopedia, but experts will check and edit the information that is submitted.

Building on the social nature of learning is another one of the keys to successful learning. Although many different classrooms focus on small collaborative groups, there is always a place for individual work and whole class instruction. Whether students work alone or with others, it is important for the teacher to foster respect for individual differences, do preassessments for flexible grouping, and make sure that students know the indicators for success so they can self-assess.

There are many developments in the fields of education, cognitive science, and neuroscience that have implications for assessment in the differentiated classroom. For example, with any learning activity it is important to provide ways of gearing up and gearing down.

SUMMARY AND CONCLUSION

However a teacher goes about assessing students, they should make learning visible for everyone involved. Self-evaluation, peer feedback, and teachers' feedback are all part of the formative assessment process. Also, everything that informs teaching can be amplified by student and teacher reflection along the path to learning and adjusting instruction.

Making assessment more authentic has a lot to do with making sure students can apply what they have learned. It also means keeping assessment close to what learners are actually doing. For example, if you are teaching the scientific method (processes), you don't assess for progress on learning narrow scientific facts.

Portfolios are part of the modern assessment package. They involve a collection of students' work that is selected to represent a variety of interests and work over a period of time. The basic idea is to collect, select, and reflect. We like using a three-ring binder for each student.

In just about every classroom, there are students who have trouble learning certain subjects. Some are motivated to learn, some aren't. A differentiated approach to assessment can help teachers identify the needs of every student and adapt instructional plans to maximize the success of each learner (Stefanakis, 2011).

Differentiated instruction has proven to be a solid asset for teachers trying to reach all students. Differentiated assessment is part of the package; it can help the instructor calculate the learning possibilities of every student. Combining differentiation with formative assessment amplifies the usefulness of both tools as teachers strive to meet specific individual and group needs in the classroom.

Assessment is much more than an examination of student work at the end of a lesson or unit of study. Academic achievement can be improved by providing frequent real-time feedback as students go about doing their work. Such formative assessment is a good example of how teachers can become aware of the students' different strengths, weaknesses, and learning styles. Also, using such a wide range of incoming information is bound to help teachers adapt and improve instruction.

As teachers more fully understand the characteristics of effective instruction, they can help the process along by designing informal formative assessment processes that examine student progress towards learning subject matter. In moving along the path to a high-quality assessment/learning environment, everyone involved can become more self-reliant, thoughtful, and motivated.

> *Language makes us human.*
> *Art and culture push the boundaries of human understanding.*
> *Science and math help us understand the natural world.*
> *Technology makes us powerful.*

And being in community with others can make us free. —D. Adams

DISCUSSION POINTS FOR TEACHERS

1. How is the brain like a parallel processor? The brain takes in sensory information and transfers it to memory. (Your digital camera takes a similar approach. Is this why memories rush in when you hear a particular song, eat a certain food, or smell an odor?)
2. Formulate a question based on sensory information (food or flowers, for example). What does your brain think of when you think of popcorn, ice cream, and so on? Write all the senses, connections you made, your emotions, the places you think of, and your personal reflections.
3. Discuss with a partner or small group your preferred learning style. Give examples.
4. Think of a subject that you've had difficulty with. Go back to the multiple intelligences. Pick one:

   Logical/mathematical: Topics that deal with day-to-day math problems in newspapers or television news.

   Verbal linguistic: How might your students use creative dramatics to act out problems drawn from science or mathematics?

   Intrapersonal: To help you develop self-understanding of any lingering science or math anxiety, use appropriate self-talk, self-analysis, and distressing techniques. Think of all the ways that you're "smart" in science or math.

   Interpersonal: After looking inside yourself, discuss the results with a partner or small group. Can you see any similarities between you and others in the group? You could do overlapping Venn diagrams (circles) that show the similarities and differences between you and others in the small group.

REFERENCES

Bailey, K., & Jakicic, C. (2012). *Common formative assessment.* Bloomington, IN: Solution Tree.

Battista, M. (2012). *Cognitive-based assessment and teaching of fractions.* Portsmouth, NH: Heinemann.

Battro, A., Fischer, K., & Lena, P. (Eds.). (2007). *The educated brain.* Cambridge, UK: Cambridge University Press.

Clarke, S. (2008). *Active learning through formative assessment.* London: Hodder Murray.

Darling-Hammond, L., Amrein-Beardsley, A., Haertel, E., & Rothstein, J. (2012). Evaluating teacher evaluation. *Phi Delta Kappan, 93*(6), 8–15.

Dweck, C. S. (2007). The perils and promises of praise. *Educational Leadership, 65*(2), 34–39.

Frey, N., & Fisher, D. (2011). *The formative assessment action plan.* Alexandria, VA: Association for Supervision and Curriculum Development.

Gardner, H. (1993). *Creating minds.* New York, NY: Basic Books.
Gardner, H. (2011). *Truth, beauty, and goodness reframed: Educating for the virtues of the twenty-first century.* New York, NY: Basic Books.
Hannaford, C. (1995). *Smart moves: Why learning is not in your head.* Arlington, VA: Great Ocean Publishers.
Jenson, E. (2005). *Teaching with the brain in mind* (2nd ed.). Alexandria, VA: Association for Supervision and Curriculum Development.
Keeley, P. (2008). *Science formative assessment: 75 practical strategies for linking assessment, instruction, and learning.* Thousand Oaks, CA: Corwin Press.
Keene, E. (2012). *Talk about understanding.* New York, NY: Teachers College Press.
Kegan, R. (2005). *Change leadership: Transforming our schools.* San Francisco, CA: Jossey-Bass.
National Academy Press. (1996). *National science education standards.* Washington, DC: National Academy Press.
National Council of Teachers of Mathematics. (2000). *Principles and standards for school mathematics.* Reston, VA: National Council of Teachers of Mathematics.
Popham, J. (2011). *Transformative assessment in action.* Alexandria, VA: Association for Supervision and Curriculum Development.
Schank, R. (2011). *Teaching minds: How cognitive science can save our schools.* New York, NY: Teachers College Press.
Stefanakis, E. (2011). *Differentiated assessment: how to access the learning potential of every student.* San Francisco, CA: Jossey-Bass.
Tomlinson, C. (2003). *Fulfilling the promise of the differentiated classroom: Strategies and tools for responsive teaching.* Alexandria, VA: Association for Supervision and Curriculum Development.
Tomlinson, C., & McTighe, J. (2006). *Integrating differentiated instruction & understanding by design: Connecting content and kids.* Alexandria, VA: Association for Supervision and Curriculum Development.
Webber, C., & Lupart, J. (Eds.). (2012). *Leading student assessment.* New York, NY: Springer-Verlag.
Wylie, E. C., et al. (2012). *Improving formative assessment practice to empower student learning.* Thousand Oaks, CA: Sage Publications.

TWO
Integrated Performance Assessments
Informative Methods for Assessing Differentiated Learning

> *In the differentiated classroom, assessment is ongoing and diagnostic. Its goal is to provide teachers day-to-day data on students' readiness for particular ideas and skills, their interests, and their learning profiles.* —Carol Tomlinson

This chapter focuses on the ongoing performance assessment techniques that teachers can use every day in their classrooms. We also give suggestions for informative assessments designed to help students show what they know. The approach is closely associated with formative assessment and portfolios (Pavri, 2012). The examples used here involve aligning assessment with differentiated scientific inquiry and mathematical problem solving. The process is both active and proactive.

Differentiated learning requires modifying instruction and designing assessments in a way that accommodates student differences. With today's increasingly diverse student body, teachers can either teach to the middle, or they can diversify their instruction and reach as many students as possible. In the differentiated classroom, instruction is based on what is known about student readiness, needs, interests, and learning profiles.

Portfolio assessment works well for differentiating learning in science and math. Portfolios require a demonstration of knowledge, skills, and understanding of the concepts or subjects being studied; the main purpose is the improvement of student learning. Like formative assessment, portfolio assessment can follow a differentiated pattern. The basic idea is to have students demonstrate what they know, are learning, or have mastered by collecting, selecting, and reflecting on multiple forms of evidence in a way that reflects a deep understanding.

Formative assessment is increasingly viewed as taking place *during* instruction. This involves the teacher gathering and acting on information about students' learning in order to improve their work while it's actually taking place. We prefer a broader definition, so we use terms such as *informative, instructional,* and *performance assessment* to more fully address multiple assessment purposes. Like formative assessment, they all match views about learning which suggest that each learner has to construct an understanding for himself or herself. The difference is giving attention to how quantitative and qualitative evidence of understanding can amplify learning before, *during*, and after instruction.

ASSESSMENT IN THE DIFFERENTIATED CLASSROOM

A blend of formative and performance assessments involves processes and strategies that can be used to collect data and gather useful information about your students. As information comes in, it is up to the teacher to make judgments. Points of view and definitions may vary, but there is general agreement that teachers are in the best position to put any data generated to good use.

Even in the most differentiated classroom, there are some assessment and curriculum issues that have to be recognized. Performing school (authorized) assessment, instructional assessment, and social assessment are among the most common assessment-related tasks for teachers.

School assessment includes grading, explaining standardized test results, and testing for special-needs placement. Instructional assessment is used to organize how and when instruction will be delivered. (For example: What textbooks or other materials will you use? How is the lesson being received? What changes have to be made in the lesson procedures?) Social assessment requires figuring out how to set up groups and enhancing communication within the class (Noyce & Hickey, 2012).

There are times when teachers can use differentiated assessment in a way that does different things for different students; such a differentiated process can stimulate learning-centered assessment. *Differentiated assessment* may be new to you. But teachers have long applied techniques such as rephrasing questions, giving a few extra examples, or extending the time allowed for a test, an activity, or a project.

From regrouping a class based on students' needs to giving assignment options, teachers have been using elements of differentiated assessment for a long time. When it comes to today's differentiated classroom, redoing assignments and class work for full credit is at least an occasional possibility.

Integrated Performance Assessments

The basic idea behind differentiated instruction is that all students, regardless of differences, should be provided with whatever it takes to reach high achievement standards. Some student suggestions include these:

- Limit the number of how do I/we do it questions.
- Talk to group members before asking the teacher if you have a problem.
- Try out discovery learning.
- When writing, speaking, and thinking, use metaphors, similes, and allegories.
- Increase your ability to work collaboratively.
- Extend your willingness to begin a task.
- Begin the questioning process.
- Summarize and combine different ideas.

UNDERSTANDING YOUR STUDENTS' ACADEMIC PROFILES

Differentiated learning and assessment begins with knowing your students. Also, teachers gather information by finding out what their students are interested in and looking for in their learning profiles. You can gather information by reviewing your students' learning backgrounds, finding out what they know, and discovering what they want to find out more about.

If your school keeps an ongoing academic record on each student, that is a good place to find out about past performance. There you will find records of standardized tests, grades, and other performance assessments. These can give you a sense about the students' strengths or limitations. You can examine the results of state assessments, look at students' learning needs, and find out what their learning styles are.

To find your students' interests both in and out of school and how they view themselves as learners, have them fill out the Student Interest Inventory (Heacox, 2002) (table 2.1).

AUTHENTIC ASSESSMENTS

Authentic assessment has a lot to do with examining evidence of the behaviors you want students to perform. For assessment to be authentic, the criterion for success must be public knowledge. Students need to know what is expected and on what criteria their work will be evaluated.

Authentic assessment is a good way to show student strengths and encourage the integration of knowledge and skills. Here are some ways to recognize authentic assessment.

- Does the students' work come from a need to solve a real problem?

Table 2.1. Student Interest Inventory

Name:	Date:

1. What is your favorite activity or subject in school? Why? Your least favorite? Why?

2. What are your "best" subjects? What makes them the easiest for you?

3. What subjects are the most difficult for you? What makes them the hardest?

4. What subject makes you think and work the hardest? Why is it the most challenging?

5. Rate the following topics according to your interests (1 = very interested, 2 = somewhat interested, 3 = not interested):

Dance =	Music =
Drama =	Sports =
Writing =	Math =
Computers =	Science =
Social studies =	Business =
World languages =	Politics/Law =

6. What are your favorite games or sports?

7. If you could learn about anything you wanted to, what would you choose to learn about? Be specific (for example, science-fiction writing, meteorology, architecture, Shakespeare, Africa, etc.).

8. What are three things you like to do when you have free time (besides seeing friends)?

9. What groups, clubs, or teams do you belong to? Include both school activities and those not sponsored by the school.

10. What careers are you currently interested in?

- Does the students' task require planning, communication, or research?
- Is the students' task unforgettable?
- Does the task have real-world connections?
- Will the task reveal the students' strengths?

- Will every student produce the same result?
- Will the task allow students to better understand their learning needs?

It is not necessary for a task to meet all of these points to be considered authentic. The important idea is that authentic assessment gives the students a sense of ownership of their learning, whereas unauthentic tasks have the feel of "doing something for the teacher." Here are some authentic activities that students can do at their desks or in a quiet corner:

1. Read a book of their choice.
2. Write an entry in their journal.
3. Keep a log of their learning experiences.
4. Use graphic organizers to help them plan.

ASSESSING WHAT'S IMPORTANT

Some methods for assessing students' growth have not kept up with recent research (Hammerman, 2008). Multiple-choice testing, for example, just doesn't do a good job of capturing the essence of today's students. Subject matter standards have changed and many of these changes are missing from the tests. Also, multiple-choice tests convey the idea to students that bits and pieces of information count more than deep knowledge.

Assessing performance is more likely to convey the notion that reasoning, in-depth understanding, taking responsibility, and applying knowledge in new situations are valued (Hales & Marshall, 2004).

Outside of school, people are usually valued for the tasks or projects they do, their ability to work with others, and the way they tackle difficult problems. Howard Gardner (1997) argued for assessment practices that "look directly at the performance that we value, whether it's a linguistic, logical, mathematical, aesthetic, or social performance." We suggest including diagnostic assessment of prior knowledge, teacher observations, student interviews, self-assessment, peer reviews, products, projects, and even the occasional quiz.

Performance portfolios are a good way to link assessment directly to instruction. Within this context, teachers and students jointly develop some important criteria for assessment.

Assessment can be used to motivate students in several ways. To begin with, students can form collaborative teams for interdisciplinary inquiry and peer assessment. As students are brought into designing assessment procedures as responsible partners, the whole process is enhanced. Students can then use portfolios to keep their own records and reflect on how well they are doing.

As learners view the evidence of their increasing proficiency, they can reflect on their own progress. By learning to communicate with peers, teachers, and parents about their achievement, learners can also learn to take more responsibility for their own academic success (Costantino, De Lorenzo, & Kobrinski, 2006).

PORTFOLIOS: COLLECTION, SELECTION, AND REFLECTION

Portfolios are a good example of performance assessment. The basic idea is to have students collect, select, reflect, and communicate what they are doing or have done. Learners think about the evidence they have collected and try to infer what it means. The process can involve peer collaboration and is a proven way to increase student involvement.

Portfolios can be used by teachers to modify or adapt instruction based on performance. As students gather evidence of progress or problems, they can adjust their own learning.

In constructing a portfolio, students use performance or work samples to show their efforts in class participation as they conduct experiments, solve problems, and participate in collaborative inquiry. Progress can be represented in a more authentic and meaningful manner. They also help teachers create performance tasks tailored to the maturity of their students and provide a framework to have conversations about the strengths and weaknesses of their students' performance.

Portfolios can be used to describe the level of performance, referred to as a "rubric" of an individual student (i.e., expert, proficient, novice, beginning). For example, the goal may be for all students to reach the proficient level by the end of fifth grade. Portfolio assessment provides individual attention to students who are making insufficient progress toward that goal.

Since portfolios capture such an authentic and visual portrait of a student's thinking and work, they are an excellent conferencing tool for meetings with students, parents, and supervisors.

STUDENT SELF-ASSESSMENT USING RUBRICS

An important element of formative assessment is feedback. For teachers, finding the time to provide feedback to every student is difficult. Students can help out by giving each other feedback. Also, self-assessment can provide an accurate source of information about the quality of their own work. This can go a long way toward judging that the goals of a lesson have been met.

Along the way to subject matter competency, peer- and self-assessment can alter the outcomes of learning for the better.

Students can access their work in progress to find ways to improve their performance. It helps if the teacher can provide a rubric or create one with their students. A rubric lists criteria and describes the varying levels of quality, from excellent to poor. When carefully designed in collaboration with students, good rubrics can provide students with clear guidelines without limiting creativity.

An Example of a Teacher-Made Rubric

1. *Set clear expectations*. Expectations should be clearly defined either by the teacher, the student, or both. List the qualities of each category. Describe several skills for each section. Descriptors should be specific. Decide on the number of points each skill is worth. This should model the state and national standards.
2. *Conduct thoughtful self-assessment*. Test the rubric with your students. Check to see whether it flows and makes sense.
3. *Revising is a crucial step*. Students need to know their efforts can lead to actual improvement opportunities. Student attitudes change with self-assessment. They tend to value it. Students reported they could self-assess effectively when they knew what the teacher expected and made attempts at revising their work.

Self-assessment can be used in any subject. If students are involved in its creation, they can assess it and improve it. A way to begin is by using the following self-assessment form.

Student Self-Assessment Form
Name:
Date:
Please answer the following questions in a thoughtful and truthful way.

1. What science or math skills are you good at now?
2. Which science or math skills would you like to be better at?
3. What could you do to improve your work in science or math?
4. Have you found more than one way to solve a problem?
5. What do you like about your work in science and math?
6. What have you learned about working with others?

After students complete the self-assessment form, their answers can be shared with other students, and their work can be edited and placed in their portfolio.

A Student/Teacher Plan for Developing Portfolios

When planning for portfolio assessment, teachers and students need to think about these questions:

1. What is the purpose of your portfolio?
2. What science/math skills will be assessed?
3. What science/math content will be included in the portfolio?
4. Who will be involved in the planning and reflecting processes?
5. How many work samples will be included?
6. Where will the portfolio be kept, and who can observe it?

Benefits of Using Portfolios

Portfolio assessments in science and math have the following advantages:

- Assessment helps make connections and communicates needs.
- Portfolios organize information and provide authentic information.
- Portfolios are an effective way to communicate with students, parents, and administrators.
- Portfolios emphasize a student's strengths and interests.
- Portfolios encourage students to assume responsibility for their learning.
- Portfolios measure student achievement over time.

When portfolios are used only for a final evaluation, student involvement will be minimal. If the purpose is to assess daily, ongoing work, students will participate in planning, selecting criteria, and evaluating their portfolios. This generates a feeling of pride and ownership for students.

When added to other performance measures, such as projects, writing assignments, presentations, and field trips, portfolios can make an important contribution to collaborative learning and differentiated instruction.

GROUPING IN THE CLASSROOM

Managing grouping strategies and making grouping decisions are important parts of every teacher's job. Learners can be brought together as a class when they need to receive directions, discuss ideas, learn new skills, or practice before a test. Students may work alone or in small groups based on their current needs. Planning for grouping requires analyzing preassessment results, arranging the classroom, and allotting time.

Students need specific directions whether they are being divided into small groups or assigned individual independent work. When learners are able to carry out activities with little adult supervision, the teacher can assess and observe students or provide direct instruction to individuals.

Flexible Grouping

Teachers plan instruction by identifying students' needs and using ongoing assessment for each individual. Flexible grouping allows students to learn information with the whole class, individually, with a partner, or in a small group. The teacher selects the grouping strategy and makes the final decision about the grouping choices.

Flexible groups try to meet the identified academic, social, and emotional needs of each student. Groups can be formed of students with similar interests, which enables them to combine their experiences and share their excitement.

An approach that combines student and teacher choice: Have students write down the three people that they would like to work with and the teacher picks one for a working partnership. If you want a group of four, just put two of the student teams together. (We suggest keeping the group size to two, three, or four.)

When student engagement involves organizing small groups, students may become more energized and enthusiastic about teamwork.

FORMATIVE ASSESSMENT SUGGESTIONS

Formative assessment is the assessment of student learning in a way that connects directly to the act of teaching. Formative instructional assessment takes place during instruction. It provides feedback to teachers and students and allows them to make adjustments that will improve their achievement and engage learners in a variety of flexible groups (Noyce & Hickey, 2012). It is important to avoid old grouping ruts by mixing up the grouping designs and making student-choice and teacher-assigned group arrangements available.

All students need to know what to expect in the classroom. When working in collaborative teams, students should try out some formative assessment strategies. For example, when studying a unit on plants with second graders, have the team divide a plant according to its parts (e.g., stem, flower, leaves, roots, etc.). Next, have them describe each part and tell how the plant uses that part.

Students can assess their learning by illustrating the plant and explaining it to a partner. This is ongoing formative assessment. Students collect information before and during the class, and then they write their observations, guesses, and thoughts about their experiences. This makes the lesson very hands-on and authentic for the students and the teacher.

Students at all grade levels can profit from formative assessment. A class of fifth graders, for example, can follow similar procedures when studying rocks. Students, in groups, try to find out which of the rocks is sedimentary, igneous, or metamorphic. They read and follow the information found in their textbook; describe each rock; examine their rocks; explain how they decided which rock characteristics belonged to each rock; discuss rock characteristics with their team; plan, compare, and test the rocks; and illustrate the rocks. (Writing and discussing are important parts of formative assessment.)

If the teacher observes a student or a group having difficulties, he or she can help that individual, small group, or the whole class. The basic idea is for the teacher to build a real-time image of a student's progress and take actions that enhance learning.

ASSESSMENT IN THE DIFFERENTIATED CLASSROOM

In a differentiated science and math classroom, teachers use any combination of tools that works to teach and assess the progress of all students. Examples include experiments, collaborative inquiry, graphic organizers, problem-solving worksheets, calculators, and concrete materials that children can manipulate to try out different numeric relationships.

From simple observation to personal portfolios, differentiated performance assessment can be used to motivate students. Points for the teacher to consider include these:

- What questions will stimulate a student's thinking the most?
- Can the students understand, organize, and systematically use the data?
- Do students comprehend the facts, concepts, and solutions to problems?
- What are the differences in the ways students present their conclusions?
- How can students improve their communication in science and math?

All teachers want students to be motivated and responsible; most believe that students should ask questions and struggle with problems to find reasonable answers.

Many teachers share a vision of what they think should be happening in their classes. This includes tailoring instruction and assessment to meet the needs of various students and clusters of students. It also includes having students work together in small groups so that they can undertake investigations and accomplish tasks. Examples of related learning tools include manipulative materials, blocks, beakers, clay, rulers, chemicals, musical instruments, calculators, assorted textbooks, computers, the Internet, and more.

ASSESSMENT AND MULTIPLE LESSON PLANNING POSSIBILITIES

There is general agreement that when teachers assess learning, they have to do more than simply test for knowledge with objective-type formats. Good assessment measures are not only the products of learning, but also the cognitive processes that are being used to produce them.

In the differentiated classroom, science and math are assessed over time—the goal is to help the student improve. Performance, thinking, and application all matter. This all has a lot to do with cognitive and metacognitive strategies—along with the mental skills required for transferring knowledge to new contexts.

Multiple-intelligences (MI) theory was developed to explain how the mind worked and how understandings were reached and applied. Ideas about educational applications came later. As has frequently been pointed out, multiple paths to understanding do not imply forming groups on the basis of different intelligence scores alone nor does it mean having eight or nine different entry points in every lesson plan.

One useful possibility related to MI theory is the concept of individual intelligence profiles. Assessment often consists of teacher observation rather than test scores. Intelligences are not isolated. Some individuals, for example, may have two strong areas with the other areas fairly weak. Other students may be more spread out along the continuum of intelligences (Chen, Moran, & Gardner, 2009).

Once teachers have some idea of a student's strengths, they can then differentiate lessons in a way that builds on that student's strengths. Sometimes the next step is making sure that a student works with a partner who has a different profile. At other times common interests might influence who comes together in a group of three or four.

ASSESSMENT CHECKLIST FOR APPLYING MULTIPLE INTELLIGENCES

Linguistic: Instruct students to use the spoken word and written communication in all of their assignments.

Logical-mathematical: Have students apply logic and use numerical symbols and operations when solving problems. They memorize the basic facts of mathematics and learn from mistakes.

Musical-rhythmic: Invite students to use musical concepts such as rhythm, pitch, melody, and harmony as they go about their daily course work. Being musical goes beyond music class; many students listen to music as often as they can. Students learn commercial jingles, move to the rhythm of a favorite musical tune, or create a song or a rap.

Spatial: Encourage students to become aware of their environment and manipulate objects in three-dimensional space. Students can create a diagram that shows the steps they take to get an answer to a science or math problem. Encourage students to make a picture or design of something they are trying to remember. Relate concepts to graphs, Venn diagrams, and branching trees. Use guided imagery to connect concepts.

Bodily-kinesthetic: Have students use movement and physical contact in their classes (for example, they may use math or science manipulatives such as a computer or math pattern blocks when explaining ideas in a science or math class). Physical movement makes learning more exciting.

Naturalist: Have learners sort and categorize objects or phenomena in nature. This is a natural process for young students.

Interpersonal: Encourage students to meet, interact, and get along with other people. Students show empathy and kindness for others and demonstrate leadership. Students participate in group situations.

Intrapersonal: Have students explain their thoughts, feelings, preferences, and interests. Students assess their work.

Existential (a relatively new possibility): Encourage students to think about questions, observations, or facts beyond sensory data, such as the infinite. Students reflect on their work.

When it comes to the assessment and planning of science/math lessons, one measure of intelligence or path to learning is far from sufficient. It's important to note that doing well in science and math involves several interacting intelligences. There are times, for example, when a strong spatial intelligence might improve a student's ability to conceptualize a mathematical concept or problem.

There are times when logical-mathematical or linguistic intelligence is the key to success. A good science or math lesson requires students to simultaneously learn along multiple dimensions. We try to build several MI points into all of our lesson plans. Again, the basic idea is to build on a student's area of strength while collaboratively addressing areas of need.

ASSESSMENT STRATEGIES FOR DIFFERENTIATED LEARNING

The National Academy of Sciences talks about five different ways for performing formative assessment: engage, explore, explain, elaborate, and assess.

- When students are engaged, they might focus on things such as current events, local issues, scientific demonstrations, experiences on a field trip, or a question that students will encounter in the unit. Connections are made between past and present learning experiences.

- When students explore, they may make observations, collect data on the Internet, or carry out investigations using laboratory equipment. Students collaboratively explain their ideas to others. They build a common base of experiences and actively explore their environment.
- When students explain, they develop explanations and use scientific terms. The content can make earlier experiences easier to describe and explain.
- When students elaborate, they extend the information into new contexts. Opportunities are given for deeper and broader understandings.
- When students assess themselves, they are encouraged to look at their understandings as they apply what they learned. They can place evidence of how they apply the information in their science/math portfolio.

PORTFOLIOS FOR TEACHER SELF-ASSESSMENT

Portfolios can help provide an ongoing conversation about processes relating to teaching and learning. They can also help us attend to subjects that don't lend themselves to traditional testing methods. Portfolios also assist in exploring what is going on *in* and *between* subjects.

The following samples are drawn from different times and contexts; they can serve as an ongoing means of getting people talking and learning across disciplines. We designed this activity for teacher self-assessment and collaborative discussion. It works just as well for prospective teachers in teacher education classes. A three-ring binder is a good way to collect things, select samples, and share reflections with other teachers. Sharing with administrators is optional.

A Teacher Self-Assessment Portfolio

Consider *your work as a whole* and select significant pieces from your notebook, readings, class experiences, and activities you have tried. Each item should encourage you to reflect on your performance and illustrate each of the categories below.

Discuss why you included each sample, how your ideas have changed over a specific period of time, and how your understanding of the subjects covered has grown with experience.

Category 1. How has your knowledge of teaching grown or changed? Include an example that reflects your growth in personal understanding and samples of activities that were meaningful to you (or that enlarged your understanding).

Category 2. How have your attitudes, beliefs, and personal confidence about educational concepts changed? Samples might include questions you raised or beliefs that you held at the beginning of the semester and a comparison with later ideas. This category may include some reflection on your views and how these attitudes will translate into your classroom practice.

Category 3. How have your experiences—in and out of the classroom—helped you understand yourself and the learning process? What have you found out about your personal learning style, strengths, weaknesses, self-esteem, and group communication skills? What does this mean for your students?

Category 4. What science/math relationships or connections do you see in your work across all subjects? Look over *all* of your notes, handouts, activities, readings, assignments, and so on, and select pieces that make meaningful connections for you—or form relationships between concepts that you have not explored before.

Category 5. How can you use what you have learned over the past year and apply it to students with special needs? Include personal insights and samples from students who are learning science and math. Compare these with samples from high-achieving students.

Linking Assessment with Instruction

Portfolios are proving useful in linking assessment with instruction at every level because they allow students and teachers to reflect on their movement through the curricular process. They also provide a chance to look at what and how students are learning while paying attention to students' ideas and thinking processes.

We do not suggest that the "objectivity" of more traditional testing has no place in the classroom. Rather, we must respect its limits and search for more connected measures of intellectual growth. But there is no question that when coupled with other performance measures, such as projects, portfolios can make an important contribution to academic success.

Rules for Assessing

1. Conduct informal, student-centered assessment in the context of learning teams. You must assess each student's achievement, but it's far more effective when it takes place in a collaborative setting. When it comes to making formal grading judgments, it is usually best to avoid group grades. However, it is important for the students to informally evaluate the work of the group itself. And remember, you want the keep the groups at two, three, or four members so that the problem of "free riders" can be minimized.

2. Offer continual feedback and assessment. Learning groups need continual informal feedback on how each member is doing. Everything from simple observations, presentations, answering questions, and oral presentations needs to be considered.
3. Develop a list of expected behaviors prior to the lesson, during the lesson, and following the lesson.
4. Directly involve students in assessing their own learning and their group work. Group members can provide immediate help to maximize all group members' learning.
5. Avoid all comparisons between students that are based solely on their academic ability. Such comparisons will decrease student motivation and learning.
6. Use a wide variety of lesson plans and assessment tools so that lessons become a vehicle for growing skill and knowledge acquisition.

DIFFERENTIATION, ASSESSMENT, AND THE SOCIAL NATURE OF LEARNING

When teachers differentiate and arrange for their students to spend significant amounts of time in learning groups, their assessment techniques change dramatically. Within this context, more emphasis is placed on student understanding and less on content recall assessed through multiple-choice tests.

When you plan for both differentiated instruction and assessment at the same time, you improve both. Assessment becomes more authentic and dynamic as it changes to reflect the changing nature of instruction in the classroom. Portfolios document performance and provide tangible evidence of learning. So it should come as no surprise to find that the content of students' portfolios can be used to guide differentiated instruction as well.

As an interactive learning/teaching tool, portfolios can help teachers with continuous formal and informal performance assessment. In the context of science and math instruction, performance may be viewed as a well-thought-out opportunity to demonstrate competency in various concepts being studied. This view of learning acknowledges the fact that students' existing thinking processes and knowledge play a major role in academic success.

Background information needs to be taken into account in teaching how to use scientific processes (i.e., the scientific method) and in developing mathematical power. Both involve more than doing scientific inquiry and giving students increasingly difficult math problems to solve. It's just as important to make sure that students are focusing on thoroughly understanding problems—and that they can explain what they are doing.

The social context of the students' performance is an important issue in teaching science, math, and just about everything else. Teachers need this information on the social dimension of learning so that they can organize mixed-ability groups in a way that reflects the amount and type of help that various students need to perform tasks.

INFORMATIVE ASSESSMENT AND ADJUSTING INSTRUCTION

By designing grouping arrangements and adjusting instruction, you will be able to include students from diverse backgrounds in challenging activities. The amount of help that children need can be adjusted by observing and analyzing the interactions that occur during the learning task. As students gain social and subject matter competence, the teacher can provide less assistance and shift more responsibility to the student groups.

Formative assessment and performance techniques (like portfolios) provide a window on student learning and classroom teaching that can't be generated by other assessment tools. They have also proven themselves useful for viewing a student's interactive skills, thinking, and competency in the subjects being studied.

When teachers share the purpose of portfolio construction with their classes, the students are more likely to see the value and relevance of selecting and reflecting on their important work. Sharing their work with others is very motivational, and everyone gains.

For teachers, sharing might involve collecting and organizing data, graphing the results, presenting a teaching strategy, and having an informal discussion of authentic assessment with a colleague. Remember, when you set out to improve something, it's important to have a goal in mind. And it is just as important to leave room for serendipity. When it comes to possibilities for improving practice, we have to be ready for chance finds.

For modern assessment practices to inform differentiated instruction, teachers can start by measuring students' understanding and level of interest. The next practical step might be to establish learning objectives by writing them on a chart entitled, "What our class wants to find out." Teachers may then introduce a variety of hands-on activities in a way that has a range of differing possibilities for every small cluster (group) of students.

Although the goal is to have all of the students reach a high standard, it is still possible for them to go about it differently. If you try to get students to learn the same things at the same time and in the same way, too many will fail to reach the objectives set for a lesson. Like formative assessments, portfolios are a natural partner for differentiated learning because everyone collects, selects, and reflects different information on the same set of skills and competencies; no two are ever done exactly the same way (Criswell, 2006).

Informed teachers hold the keys to the future. Activating rich classroom experiences depends upon the teacher's ability to figure out a student's prior experiences, developmental needs, personal preferences, and the level of competency involved in the subject being studied. Another key ingredient: good assessment tools that inform instruction in a way that supports the achievement of instructional goals.

SUMMARY AND CONCLUSION

Teaching, learning, and assessment are intimately connected. At their best, formative assessment and portfolios require students to demonstrate the desired procedure or skill in a realistic context. Such techniques allow students—or teachers, for that matter—to display growing strengths rather than simply expose weaknesses.

By connecting more authentic assessment to differentiated instruction, teachers promote student ownership of learning. And by encouraging students to use, shape, and reflect on what knowledge is most important, they can amplify both assessment and instruction (Barell, 2012).

When it comes to pedagogical change, informal belief systems are just as important as methodology. In many ways, the thoughtful reflection about practice that comes with modern assessment practices and differentiated instruction can play a major role in helping teachers become more effective professionals.

Generating the energy to act on new practices is an art. It has a lot to do with understanding human nature, establishing a readiness for change, and developing an intellectual understanding of new possibilities. The most effective innovations are usually research based and classroom friendly. Change is a personal process. So making changes in curriculum and assessment without involving teachers is a contradiction in terms.

To move quality instruction and assessment from talk to action requires the involvement of informed teachers who can make good use of new concepts. In addition, teachers must be involved in educational decision making about curriculum, instruction, and assessment. If their voices are left out, then our schools will miss the important improvement opportunities provided by innovations like formative assessment, differentiated instruction, and portfolio assessment (Abell & Volkmann, 2006).

It is too easy to blame teachers for parental and societal shortcomings. Bringing the nation's educational system up to international standards requires talented teachers. But it also requires the reduction of child poverty, a full curriculum, and raising the status of the teaching profession (Ravitch, 2010).

The quality of assessment and instruction is so much more than test scores; what matters most is teaching with creativity and passion.

Professionals don't blossom when they spend their careers enfolded in the logic of others. Teachers themselves are in the best position to identify the key issues and questions, probe, assess, and try to attain clarity. They are also the ones who can implement differentiated learning in the sometimes ambiguous world of curriculum and instruction.

As teachers become students of their own learning, they can discover the inconsistencies between what they believe about gaining knowledge and how they practice teaching. After all, the discoveries we make for ourselves are more convincing and make us more willing to change what we do.

> *I believe that we should get away altogether from tests and correlations among tests and look instead at more naturalistic sources of information about how peoples around the world develop skills important to their way of life.* — Howard Gardner

DISCUSSION POINTS FOR TEACHERS

1. How do *you* think you do when it comes to the subjects of science and math? Write down the major points that you can remember about how your scientific and mathematical abilities have been assessed. What did these assessments tell you about your ability in these subjects?
2. A great deal of assessment should be based on observations of students engaging in science and math. How might you do a better job of situating assessment in real (authentic) classroom learning?
3. A portfolio is a selection of in-progress and completed student work; it encourages you to use many different ways to think about and assess student progress. By their very nature, portfolios require collaboration between student and teacher. How could portfolios help you do a better job of taking into account the diversity of student backgrounds, learning needs, and culture?
4. How could you do a better job of balancing the assessment of students' learning with the instructional goals of your curriculum?

REFERENCES

Abell, S., & Volkmann, M. (2006). *Seamless assessment in science: A guide for elementary and middle school teachers*. Portsmouth, NH: Heinemann.

Barell, J. (2012). *How do we know they're getting better?: Assessment for 21st century minds, K8*. Thousand Oaks, CA: Corwin Press.

Borich, G., & Tombari, M. (2004). *Educational assessment for elementary and middle school education*. Upper Saddle River, NJ: Pearson Education.

Chen, J., Moran, S., & Gardner, H. (Eds.) (2009). *Multiple intelligences around the world.* San Francisco, CA: Jossey-Bass.

Costantino, P., De Lorenzo, M., & Kobrinski, E. (2006). *Developing a professional teaching portfolio: A guide for success* (2nd ed.). Boston, MA: Allyn & Bacon.

Criswell, J. (2006). *Developing assessment literacy: A guide for elementary and middle school teachers.* Norwood, MA: Christopher-Gordon Publishers.

Gardner, H. (1997). Multiple intelligences as a partner in school improvement. *Educational Leadership, 55*(1), 20–21.

Hales, L., & Marshall, J. (2004). *Developing effective assessments to improve teaching and learning.* Norwood, MA: Christopher-Gordon Publishers.

Hammerman, E. (2008). *Formative assessment strategies for enhanced learning in science.* Thousand Oaks, CA: Corwin Press.

Heacox, D. (2002). *Differentiating instruction in the regular classroom: How to reach and teach all learners, grades 3–12.* Minneapolis, MN: Free Spirit Publishing.

Montgomery, K. (2000). *Authentic assessment: A guide for elementary teachers.* Boston, MA: Addison-Wesley.

Noyce, P., & Hickey, D. (2012). *New frontiers in formative assessment.* Cambridge, MA: Harvard University Press.

Pavri, S. (2012). *Effective assessment of students: Determining responsiveness to instruction.* Toronto, Ontario, Canada: Pearson Education Canada.

Ravitch, D. (2010). *The death and life of the great American school system: How testing and choice are undermining education.* New York, NY: Basic Books.

Tomlinson, C. (1999). *The differentiated classroom: Responding to the needs of all learners.* Alexandria, VA: Association for Supervision and Curriculum Development.

Tomlinson, C. (2008). Learning to love assessment. *Educational Leadership, 65*(4), 8–13.

Wormmeli, R. (2006). *Fair isn't always equal: Assessing and grading in the differentiated classroom.* Portland, ME: Stenhouse.

www.assessmentinst.com and www.makingstandardswork.com are two websites we often use to explore assessment issues and practices.

THREE

Science Instruction

Inquiry, Teamwork, and Informative Assessment

> *When you open your science classroom to inquiry-based learning you must align your curriculum to assessment strategies that mirror the investigatory spirit, rather than rely on traditional, end-of-unit tests that eschew process for product.* —Abell and Volkmann

Sometimes science-based ideas and concepts are new to the individual. At other times, it is a question of expanding knowledge that has not been fully explored. Either way, inquiry is at the center of science instruction. It is more than a set of procedures or skills associated with the scientific method. The inquiry skills of science are acquired through questioning and becoming engaged in authentic investigation and problem solving.

Science education is a lot more than just piling up information. Certainly, learning how to discover information and knowledge is important. But the ability to sort through the flood of information and synthesize the best ideas is crucial. The same can be said for personal development and being able to self-assess; both have a lot to do with students coming to understand themselves as learners of science (Ellis, 2010).

The best way for learners to understand scientific inquiry is to actually do it. Social development and teamwork skills influence the nature of classroom inquiry. The quality of group interaction also has a lot to do with the level of discussion, leadership, and peer assessment. We try to enhance the process by presenting some ideas, activities, and assessment techniques.

The collaborative science activities here are classroom tested and built on the scientific processes of inquiry, discovery, and problem solving. The lesson plans and assessment suggestions are arranged in a way that allows teachers to reach across the curriculum. And, as you will see, the differentiated small-group activities have been influenced by the science standards.

Formative assessment can improve scientific inquiry by providing useful information (gathered along the way) that can inform instruction as the student progresses and the curriculum unfolds. This takes place over time, so it won't help as much with a short forty-five-minute lesson.

Summative assessment can be used to make end-of-lesson judgments about the value, worth, and effectiveness of classroom learning experiences. Portfolios, a type of performance assessment, can also be summative. They also leave plenty of room for self, peer, and differentiated teacher feedback.

No matter what the classroom evaluation mix is, the closer student assessment is aligned with curriculum and instruction, the more likely it is to provide an accurate picture of learning and amplify academic achievement.

EXAMPLES FROM THE SCIENCE FRAMEWORK

Inquiry, team learning, and modern assessment are closely associated ways of making sure that all students learn the processes and principles of science. Collaborative inquiry in science builds on the social nature of learning and ensures that science instruction is meaningful and exciting for struggling students, without slowing down those who are doing really well.

In 2011, the National Research Council (NRC) introduced *A Framework for K–12 Science Education Practices.* It examined important concepts all students should learn. The framework builds an outline for the new science standards that are replacing the standards of the 1990s (National Research Council, 2011).

One of the most important ideas is that children can be investigators even in the early grades. The basic idea is that all students should engage in scientific and engineering practices. The framework also suggests paying close attention to the core ideas of science and their real world applications.

At any level, science and engineering require knowledge, practice, and a focus on students' interests and experiences (Pratt, 2012).

COLLABORATIVE INQUIRY IN SCIENCE

When students are engaged in collaborative inquiry, they work together to accomplish shared goals. Although the group sinks or swims together, there is individual accountability. It is up to the teacher to ensure that students focus on important understandings and skills so that they don't get swamped in a mire of disjointed facts.

As science lessons progress, it is usually best for the teacher to support advanced learners by getting them involved with more complex problems. Unless the context is changed, just having more advanced learners go back over what they already know is not all that useful. Personal growth and individual success matter, so does giving every student a chance to find science meaningful and interesting.

The research suggests that collaborative inquiry can result in better student questions and a clearer picture of science content (Marzano, 2010). When learners explore topics that are of special interest to them, they become motivated, even those who would rather avoid learning about science or math. Whatever the problem, subject, or issue, inquiry is at its best when students use thinking skills that are similar to those used by scientists who are searching for new knowledge in their field (Etheredge & Rudnitsky, 2003).

It should be noted that when teams of actual scientists are testing new ideas, the result is often two papers forward, followed by a one-paperback intellectual disagreement by a competing team of scientists. No wonder the public sometimes gets journalistic whiplash as reporters with little or no science background careen from one extreme to the other.

When students meaningfully apply scientific inquiry skills, it will go a long way toward helping them understand how the growth of scientific understanding is built on reasoned disagreements and certain accepted principles. It is also important to be able to deal with the ambiguities that often precede the tipping point of overwhelming evidence in support of a new advance.

When it comes to science assignments, it is sometimes best to follow the classical approach: Don't tell your students *how* to do something. Tell them *what* to do and let them surprise you with their ingenuity. It is not the teacher's job to tell students what to think. Rather it is best to draw them toward a feeling of wonder about the natural world.

Teachers may guide and coach their students through the kinds of inquiry activities that help them build an understanding of the typical scientific journey toward a better understanding of how the world works. Along the way, they can give students a degree of ownership as they plan and organize some of the class activities together. The teacher may also share some of the leadership by inviting students to be part of the planning and teaching process.

When learners teach one another, everyone usually learns more. Effective teachers sometimes go one step further and involve students in discussions about class rules, schedules, and teaching procedures. The result is that inquiry can go beyond science to provide students with valuable insights about themselves and the nature of teamwork.

CONSTRUCTING KNOWLEDGE IN ASSOCIATION WITH OTHERS

Students can flourish when good teaching is combined with collaborative inquiry and an engaging curriculum (Tomlinson, 1999). Collaborative inquiry generally involves asking questions, observing, examining information, investigating, arriving at answers, and communicating the results. A collaborative inquiry approach to the teaching of science has been found to work well with all learners.

It adds enthusiasm to the subject when students experience the excitement of science in small groups. Knowledge of science has always been constructed in association with others. Science is much more than an individual endeavor. As with other elements of science instruction, it's best if students of all ages employ procedures that have some resemblance to those that scientists actually use (Rosenzweig, 2011).

The collaborative inquiry approach is student centered. The teacher often gives the students directions and materials, but does not tell the small group exactly how to go about doing its work. (Remember the "don't tell them *how* to do things" maxim.) The teacher encourages conversation and provides activities that help students understand how science is applied in the world outside of school.

For example: As students connect with materials and their peers, they can interact with science or math problems and jointly recognize the results of their investigation. Also, differentiated lessons can encourage learners to pursue topics of interest in a way that enhances their curiosity.

Students certainly have different talents and interests, but they should all have access to high-quality science instruction. Differentiated instruction, collaborative experiences, and concrete materials can motivate even the most reluctant learner—especially one who is having trouble with basic science or math skills.

Since motivation is often a major concern, it is necessary to go beyond rote skill building to challenge all learners. Being stuck in a remedial basic skills class is a recipe for disaster. This means helping each and every student spend at least some time with interesting, difficult, and ambiguous problems where the student is expected to discuss, question, and resolve problems.

COLLABORATION, INQUIRY, AND SCIENCE LEARNERS

Inquiry is sometimes thought of as the way people study the world and propose explanations based on the evidence they've accumulated. It involves actively seeking information, truth, and knowledge. When collaboration is added to the process, it helps build the positive relationships that are at the heart of a learning community.

Collaborative inquiry may be thought of as a range of concepts and techniques for enhancing interactive questioning, investigation, and learning. When questions that connect to student experiences are raised collectively, ideas and strengths are shared in a manner that supports the students' search for understanding (Snow, 2005).

Teachers have found that using a collaborative approach in science instruction is a way to involve uninterested students in active small-group learning. When students work together as a team, they tend to motivate one another. Accomplishing shared goals benefits all of the individuals in a group and makes it more likely that collaboration will become a natural part of the fabric of instruction.

When it comes to collaborative learning, the teacher provides a high degree of structure in forming groups and defining procedures, but students control the interactions within their groups. Building team-based organizational structures in the classroom makes it easier for teachers to reach out to students who have problems and ensure that all students are successful.

A shift in values and attitudes may be required for a collaborative learning environment to reach its full potential. Some traditional school environments have conditioned students to rely on the teacher to validate their thinking and direct learning.

Getting over years of learned helplessness takes time. Students need to be actively engaged and feel in charge of their learning. Whether they're third graders or middle-school students, most students want to help the teacher with classroom chores.

One way to get students involved is to form a planning group session to assist the teacher and help students assume a leadership role. At the beginning of the year, the teacher announces that he or she needs some help in planning for the science and math classes. The teacher excitedly explains that all students will be involved. A chart is created with nine months and spaces for the names of each student.

Students have a chance to decide which month they will choose to be a planning group leader. Group leaders are responsible for coming to the planning group session during the month that they are the leader of a small group. The teacher's job is to get students excited about their shared leadership role and make sure that they understand the purpose and structure of the lessons that they will be working with (Rhoton & Bowers, 2001).

PLANNING GROUP DIRECTIONS FOR STUDENTS

Students will sign up for a planning group session that meets over the course of one month. In each session, students will meet with the teacher and help plan the class sessions. Planning group students will be the leader of their group for the month. The planning group sessions might take place during recess or free time, when the rest of the class is not present. Directions or materials can be given to them to take home so that they have a chance to think about what's coming up.

Planning Group Jobs

1. Help organize materials for the class.

    Get materials from classroom cupboards/shelves.
    Organize the tables and chairs for the class.
2. Get directions from the teacher for the activities to be done in class.
3. Try out the activities the class will be doing with other planning group members.
4. Discuss ideas, questions, or changes you feel would be useful.
5. Discuss with the planning group members:

    Any questions you feel students in the class may have.
    Any items that need to be made clearer.
    How you will divide up the class into groups.
6. Prepare learning materials.

The teacher explains the directions to the class.

INQUIRY SKILLS THAT ADDRESS STUDENT NEEDS

Inquiry builds on the *what* of science to pay close attention to the *how*. At its best, it is driven by meaningful and authentic questions. In addition, classroom inquiry frequently embeds instruction in a context of small-group work that encourages cooperative exploration and application of a basic body of knowledge. For the teacher, knowing the level of prior understanding is important because the basic idea is to help learners develop the attitudes and skills they need to build a foundation for future discoveries.

Being able to use the knowledge and skills of science in meaningful ways is an important objective for everyone. Meaningful learning means giving students some active control over the content they learn as well as giving them the possibility of using what they have learned in a personal way. So it is a good idea to have learners manipulate objects, adapt ideas, and create personal knowledge through interesting small-group experiences. Along the way, they have a good chance of developing an appreciation for the rules and principles that guide the inquiry process.

All subjects are built upon important concepts and principles that demand the use of the necessary skills. When planning for the class lesson, the teacher should have a specific list of what each student should know, understand, and be able to do. Then the teacher creates a variety of engaging and exciting activities to help all students accomplish these skills.

To be effective, teachers must ensure that lessons are built on the curiosity of children as well as on curriculum content (Carin, Bass, & Contant, 2005). As learners construct knowledge (or "process," as Piaget calls it), they make science and mathematics relevant and personal. Teachers should introduce and plan class inquiry discussions and activities that address each skill.

Observing

The most important tool for students is observation. Wanting to find out about their world makes students eager to explore and ask questions. Observing involves using all the senses: seeing, hearing, tasting, smelling, and feeling—working together to gather as much information as possible. Observations are the foundation for all other inquiry skills. Students should be directed to describe what they see, hear, smell, touch, and, perhaps, taste. Encourage passive learners to try and provide some specific measurements of their observations. Most times, even reluctant learners are motivated and excited about what they observe.

Sorting and Classifying

Students learn about objects by grouping and ordering them. As students become more skilled in recognizing characteristics of objects, they learn to recognize likenesses and differences between objects. At a young age, students are able to classify or sort objects into groups by color, size, or shape; rearrange the set; and put the groups in some kind of order. Even students who have difficulty remembering are not daunted by sorting and classifying objects.

Comparing

Once students learn to observe and describe objects, they soon begin to compare two or more objects. Students may say they want more or fewer; they can tell you what is the same or different. Being able to compare individual objects and sets will help students decide whether four is more or less than six. Comparing is not just a skill for students in the early grades. Students will use this skill in every grade and throughout their work in every discipline.

Sequencing

Students live with sequences and patterns. They may notice patterns in nature such as the symmetry of a leaf or the wings of an insect. They can observe patterns in buildings, such as the ways bricks fit together or the markings on the floor. Sequencing is finding or bringing order to their observations. The patterns that exist all around students are enlivened when teachers direct students' observations and pattern-finding activities.

Measuring

Active experiences in science and math provide many opportunities to describe and compare in terms of quantity. Young students automatically use numbers when comparing quantities—one student is taller than another, one backpack is heavier, one ball is larger, and so forth. Active measuring experiences in science and math provide many opportunities for struggling learners to describe and compare in terms of quantity.

Measuring supplies the hard data necessary to confirm hypotheses and make predictions. It provides firsthand information. Measuring includes gathering data on size, weight, and quantity. Measurement tools and skills have a variety of uses in everyday adult life. Being able to measure connects science and math to the environment.

Using Space-Time Relationships

As students compare, classify, and sequence objects, they soon look at relationships among the objects. Relationships are rules or agreements used to associate one or more objects or concepts with another. Science and math are collections of relationships among objects or concepts. A concept in nature is that animals have certain needs—air, food, water, and space.

A variety of factors affects the ability of animals to maintain their survival over time. Everything in natural systems is interrelated. If one of these needs were eliminated, the animal population would dwindle and die. In mathematics, there are many examples of relationships. Ideas such as six, triangle, ones/tens/hundreds (as in place value), sum, product, ratio, and equivalent are all examples of relationships.

Communicating

Communication stresses the importance of being able to talk about, write about, describe, and explain science or math ideas. Symbolism, along with visual aids such as charts and graphs, should become ways of expressing science and math ideas to others. This means that students should learn not only to interpret the language of science and math, but also to use that language both in and beyond the classroom.

Young people are in the process of discovering who and what they are. It is necessary for them to form some positive impressions of themselves based on sound observations and evidence. All learners benefit as they come to realize that they are not alone in having problems with science and mathematics.

Students gain by regularly talking, writing, drawing, graphing, and using symbols, numbers, and tables to help them think about and communicate their ideas (Campbell & Fulton, 2003). These formative assessments can provide students with the necessary feedback and help teachers identify the concepts that students have not mastered.

Using Data

The disciplines of science and mathematics identify statistics and probability as important links to many content areas. The skills of data gathering, analyzing, recording, using tables, and reading graphs provide many opportunities for representing, interpreting, and recording that apply many science and math concepts and skills.

Many decisions are based on market research and sales projections, for instance. If these data are to be understood and used, all people should be able to process such information efficiently. For example, consider the science/math concepts involved in the following:

- Weather reports—decimals, percentages, probability, observing weather patterns, classifying climate zones, identifying weather fronts, and so on.
- Public opinion polls—sampling techniques and errors of measurement.
- Advertising claims—hypothesis testing, product research, polls, sales records, projections, and so on.
- Monthly government reports involving unemployment, inflation, and energy supplies.

All media depend on techniques for summarizing information. Radio, television, the Internet, and newspapers bombard us with statistical information. The current demand for information-processing skills continues to grow. Teachers can provide a tape or CD that struggling students can listen to several times as they try to complete difficult statistical tasks.

Graphing

Graphing skills include constructing and reading graphs as well as interpreting graphical information. They should be introduced in the early grades. The data should depend on children's interest and maturity.

Here are a few kinds of survey data that could be collected in the classroom:

- Physical characteristics—height, eye color, shoe size
- Sociological characteristics—birthdays, number of children in the family
- Personal preferences—favorite television shows, favorite books, favorite sports, favorite food

Each of these concepts gives students the opportunity to collect data themselves (Hassan, 2012). Graphic messages can provide a large amount of information at a glance. In creating a graph, it is important to make the graph large enough for students to manipulate and make interpretations, predictions, or analyses.

Using Language

Language is a window into students' thinking and understanding. For most individuals, oral language is the primary means of communication. One of the overriding objectives in the collaborative classroom is to facilitate the use of oral language and listening as different means of communication and learning.

Language reveals the quality of the students' science and math communication. Listening to students' language is a valuable way to get feedback from students' efforts. There are many ways to give students opportunities to practice and use language effectively (Strickland, Ganske, & Monroe, 2002). Effective communication will, of course, depend not only on topical knowledge, but also on the students' ability to communicate orally. Self-awareness also fits in—how well are students applying their oral communication skills?

There are many different ways to involve students actively in the language learning process. A few are mentioned here: storytelling, directed reading activities, art (clay modeling, drawing, sculpture), music (playing, singing, listening), oral presentations, small-group discussions, and creative dramatics.

Sharing

The process of sharing helps students feel more comfortable and less inhibited in speaking before an audience. Sharing allows students to develop independence and to share their work and ideas. Again, self-confidence is very important. Whole-class discussions are held after the children have had time to explore a particular activity or idea. Teachers use these group sharing times to summarize and interpret data from explorations. Group sharing is a time for students to discuss their ideas, focus on math and science relationships, and help learners make connections among activities.

Predicting

Students learn that not all predictions are accurate. Often, there is a high degree of uncertainty in predicting. The ability to make predictions is based on skillful observation, inference, quantification, and communication. Students who understand predicting are aware that unforeseen events can change the conditions of a prediction and that 100 percent accuracy is not likely.

Estimating

The curriculum should include estimation so that students can explore estimation strategies, recognize when an estimation is appropriate, determine the reasonableness of results, and apply estimation in working with quantities, measurement, computation, and problem solving (NCTM, 2000).

Inferring

The basic process skill of inference involves making conclusions based on reasoning. Children often make inferences about their observations. Observations and inferences are directly related. Inferences are based on observations and experiences. Students are often very creative in making inferences based on what they have observed. Inferences extend observation by allowing learners to explain their findings and predict what they think will happen.

Discussing important terms and writing about them help those students who may be confused by the vocabulary. Language is a powerful tool for gathering and sharing information. Students are encouraged to talk with teachers, other adults, and one another while they are engaged in observing and making inferences based on their senses and experiences.

The basic inquiry processes just discussed are global in their application—not limited to math and science investigation. For example, students might use the process of inferring why their teacher was pleased (or annoyed) with them in class yesterday. Another example might be sorting and classifying their supplies for an upcoming field trip.

SCIENCE INQUIRY ACTIVITIES

Differentiation comes naturally because inquiry strategies are based on the idea that teachers consider student differences when they set up mixed-ability groups.

The following are some classroom-tested teaching strategies influenced by the science standards for elementary and middle-school learners.

1. Observe and Describe Using the Five Senses

Description: This activity uses the five senses. The process skills of observing, inferring, communicating (sharing), and hypothesizing are introduced.

Objectives:

1. Students will observe and make inferences with their senses.
2. Students will talk and share their ideas with others.
3. Students will ask questions and make hypotheses based on their senses.
4. Students will verify their thinking through personal experiences.

Planning group: Members should arrange the classroom and materials.
Procedures:

1. Select several objects that are safe to touch, smell, and taste (cookies, an orange, an apple, and popcorn are good choices).
2. Put one object in a clean paper bag and ask students to feel the object without looking inside.
3. Have students describe what they feel.
4. Have students smell the object without peeking.
5. Encourage students to describe what they smell.
6. Shake the bag and invite students to describe what they hear.
7. Next, you may wish to have students taste the object and describe it.
8. Finally, allow students to look at the object and verify their guesses.

It's important for students to discuss the strategies they used in making their guesses. Point out the invaluable role of others. Ask what they learned from other classmates about making inferences. Experiences such as these give students an opportunity to develop and refine many science and math concepts.

Students may use vague or emotional terms rather than specific descriptive words. It's important to discuss the communication process since words are most effective in describing what they did. Let students discuss which words give better descriptions. Have students relate their everyday language to science and math language and symbols.

Evaluation: Have students share their experiences through language and cultural anecdotes. Language materials designed to teach non-English-speaking students are valuable when helping all students.

2. *What Do You See?*

Description: This group-centered activity involves the process skills of observing, inferring, measuring, comparing, ordering by distance, formulating conclusions, and recording.

Objectives:

1. Students will be able to observe and record data accurately.
2. Students will use simple scientific equipment.
3. Students will demonstrate the ability to work in groups in an organized and productive manner.

Process skills: Measuring, comparing, inferring, ordering by distance, and formulating conclusions.

Planning group: Members should arrange the classroom and materials.

Materials:

1. Five samples: a housefly, a computer disk, a flower, a piece of fabric, and a sample of paper (other samples may be substituted for those listed)
2. Twelve magnifying glasses
3. Six rulers
4. An observation sheet for each student

Procedures:

1. Six stations, each including two magnifying glasses, one of the samples listed above, and a ruler are set up around the room.
2. Each student receives an observation sheet.
3. Students are divided into six groups of four students each.
4. Each group is assigned a station. At this station, the group has ten minutes to record as many observations about the sample as possible.
5. Each student in the group, while using the magnifying glass and the ruler, makes an observation for the group to record. Students take turns as time allows.
6. As a class, students compare and discuss their observations.
7. Students are actively involved whether they're the group leader or part of the team. If students have difficulty, encourage them to work together as a partnership.

Evaluation: Data sheets are evaluated on organization, observation skills, and accuracy.

3. Science/Math Nature Search

Description: Science and mathematics applications are all around us. Mathematical patterns in nature abound. Architecture, art, and everyday objects rely heavily on science and mathematical principles, patterns, and symmetrical geometric forms. Students need to see and apply real-world connections to concepts in science and mathematics. This activity is designed to get students involved and more aware of the scientific/mathematical relationships all around them and use technology to help report their findings. This activity requires students to use the process skills of observation, classification, comparison, sequence, measurement, and communication.

Objectives:

1. Students will participate in observing, communicating, and collecting samples.
2. Students will exhibit their understanding by recording their observations in their notebooks.
3. Students will show their ability to work in groups in a responsible, interactive, and productive manner.
4. Students will reflect their thinking orally and in writing.

Planning group: Members should arrange the classroom and materials.

Procedures: Divide the class into four groups. Each group is directed to find and bring back as many objects as they can that meet the requirements on their list. Some objects may need to be sketched out on paper if they are too difficult to bring back to the classroom, but encourage students to try to bring back as many as possible.

Group One: Measurement Search

Process skills: Measuring, comparing, inferring, ordering by distance, formulating conclusions.

Procedure: Find and bring back objects that are

As wide as your hand
A foot long
Farther away than you can throw
Waist high
Half the size of a baseball
As long as your arm
Smaller than your little finger
Wider than four people
Thinner than a shoelace

As wide as your nose
(If it's too big, just report about it.)

Group Two: Shape Search

Process skills: Comparing shapes, recognizing patterns, recording data.
Procedure: Find and bring back as many objects as you can that have these shapes and record them in your notebook:

Triangle
Oval
Circle
Rectangle
Square
Hexagon
Diamond
Other geometric shapes

Group Three: Number Pattern Search

Process skills: Comparing numbers, shapes, and patterns; recording data.
Procedure: Find objects that show number patterns. For example, a three-leaf clover matches the number pattern three.

Group Four: Texture Search

Process skills: Observing, collecting, classifying, recording data, comparing, and labeling.
Procedures: Find as many objects as you can that have the following characteristics:

Smooth
Bumpy
Rough
Furry
Soft
Sharp
Grooved/ridged
Wet
Hard
Grainy

Evaluation: When students return, have them arrange their objects in some type of order or classification. Using a graphing program on the computer, or colored paper, scissors, and markers, have them visually represent their results in some way (using a bar graph, for example).

4. Boxes Revealing Identity

Description: Just what do we mean when we talk about identity? This activity tries to answer that question. Identity is your personality, friends and family, talents and abilities, the place you live now, and the place from which you came. It's the thing that makes you proud; it is expressed in your clothes, music, works of art, writings, photos, books, memories, and hopes for the future. This activity is designed to awaken students to the value of themselves and to share and communicate who and what they are.

Objectives:

1. Students will define and discover what identity means for them.
2. Students will create autobiographies in small rectangular boxes with hinged lids (a shoe box is a good example).
3. Through writing exercises, time lines, and visual webs of important things in their lives, students will gather artifacts to put in their boxes.
4. Students will display their boxes in a class gallery exhibit and share their feelings.
5. Through drawings and writing, the students will not only respond to their own boxes, but also reflect upon what they learned about others.

Process skills: Communicating, analyzing, discovering relationships, solving problems, collecting data, testing predictions, constructing, valuing, and reflecting.

Planning group: Members should arrange the classroom and materials.

Procedures:

1. Collect as many objects as you can that reveal your identity.
2. Construct a time line or visual map of important things in your life.
3. Gather artifacts (pictures, maps of important places, toys, hobbies, sports memorabilia, baby teeth, lucky rocks, etc.) to put in your box.
4. Brightly colored paper, "glitz" from silver and gold contact paper, small mirrors, colored pencils, and markers also add excitement.
5. Create your autobiographies and express your ideas/feelings in writing.
6. Construct your project.

Evaluation: Through drawing and writing, have students respond to their own boxes and reflect upon what they learned from others. Students display and present their projects.

5. Magnet Attraction

Description: Given a set of materials and a magnet, groups of students will predict and then test whether or not the objects will be/are attracted to the magnet. Students will record their findings and hypothesize (or "guess") why some objects are attracted while others are not.

Objectives:

1. Students will predict which objects are magnetic.
2. Students will test the objects they have identified as magnetic.
3. Students will record their findings in their journals.
4. Groups will review and discuss their findings with the class, sharing their discoveries, and comparing results with other groups.
5. Students will actively participate in their groups. Each student will learn that magnets attract certain metal objects—iron and steel.

Process skills: Describing, predicting, experimenting, forming hypotheses, testing predictions, recording data, inferring, and recognizing cause-and-effect relationships.

Planning group: Members should arrange the classroom and materials.

Background information: Before conducting this activity, students should vaguely know what a magnet is—that it attracts (or sticks to) certain objects. Magnets attract only certain objects. Not all objects made of metal are attracted to the magnet. Objects made of iron or steel are attracted to the magnet.

Materials:

1. A sack or brown bag (to hold objects to test).
2. A magnet (large enough for students to handle with ease) and paper or notebook.
3. Approximately twenty objects (about half of which will be attracted to the magnet). Examples of objects:

Tacks	Rubber bands
Paper clips	Pebbles
Needles	Wood
Pencils	Glass
Screws	Cloth
Nails	Pieces of sponge
Pins	Chalk
Coins	Paper
Copper	Plastic
Aluminum	Leather

Procedures:

1. Divide students into groups of three, four, or five.
2. Present this problem to the class: Which of these objects are magnetic?
3. Assign jobs, or have students determine jobs themselves (supply getter, record keeper, object displayer [from bag], and cleanup person).
4. Before letting students get their supplies, explain to students that each group will be given a magnet and a bag of objects.
5. Students will view their objects one at a time, predict whether or not it will be attracted to the magnet, and then test the object. Both predictions and results should be recorded in their notebook.
6. After the objects have been tested, students should review and discuss their findings and answer the following questions:

    What do the objects that were attracted to the magnet have in common?
    What do the objects that were not attracted have in common?
    What can you conclude from your investigation?

7. Groups of students will see how many objects they can find in the classroom that are attracted to their magnets.
8. Students will keep a list of all the things that are attracted to their group's magnet.
9. Students will share their group's findings with the class.
10. Students will compare and discuss what other groups found out.

Evaluation: Group written work along with oral discussion will provide feedback as to whether or not students are understanding the concept of magnetism. If students are confused, encourage them to work with their group. Direct students to write what they learned about magnetism. Have them reflect on their group's process, expressing their knowledge as well as their impressions about this "magical" thing called magnetism.

FORMATIVE/SUMMATIVE ACTIVITIES

Corrective activities present the concepts in a different way. They engage students in various learning situations and provide students with rewarding experiences. Giving students a chance to learn a science or math concept in a new way with different paths to learning adapted to meet individual learning needs and interests invites success. A few corrective activities may include:

- Reteaching—The teacher explains a concept again using a different approach and different examples.

- Peer tutoring—Students who have already mastered the material often make excellent tutors for their fellow classmates. Encourage students to volunteer to be tutors.
- Collaborative teams—In collaborative teams, two to five students get together to discuss their learning difficulties and to help one another. During the corrective session, student teams go over the formative assessment item by item. Team members work collaboratively to find a solution.
- Alternative textbooks—When available, alternative textbooks provide a different presentation than the class textbook. A new way of seeing an old concept is a welcome corrective addition.
- Academic games and learning kits—Learning games and kits promote collaboration and can be highly effective corrective activities.
- Computer technology activities—Frequently, teachers use computers, videodiscs, and interactive video for teaching corrective activities.

These formative and summative assessment tools offer teachers an exciting way to improve student learning. Involving students in corrective activities and challenging well-designed assessments makes differentiated learning a very practical way to help all students succeed.

Effective assessment identifies areas needing improvement and suggests a plan of action. And feedback is most effective when it presents understandable information about student performance that can be used to improve learning. Action plans may include reteaching an important concept, peer tutoring, working in collaborative teams, and using alternative textbooks, academic games, learning kits, and online activities.

Science is a system of knowing about the universe—large and small, near and far. Instruction in the subject is designed to expand students' perceptions and appreciation of nature—water, rocks, plants, animals, people, and other elements in the world around us and beyond.

What and *how* we teach children and young adults have to be at the top of the national agenda. To compete in a globalized world, any society must rank science, mathematics, and technology among its highest priorities (Golden & Katz, 2008). As far as the classroom is concerned, teachers need to cultivate the quality of their students' scientific reasoning so that they can recognize the importance of backing up science-related arguments with reliable information and solid data.

As subject-matter understanding and related reasoning skills develop in students, these skills are bound to build self-reliance and confidence as well. It doesn't stop at the science lesson. The intellectual tools of science give students abilities that can be used in versatile and productive ways across disciplines.

SUMMARY AND CONCLUSION

Here we have used examples drawn from science education to illustrate inquiry process skills. These include observing, classifying, inferring, measuring, comparing, sequencing, communicating, predicting, recording, investigating, and experimenting. By experiencing these processes, it is our belief that all learners can feel the power of creating their own knowledge and validating their own accomplishments.

Scientific inquiry requires much more than shifting sources of information to reinforce existing views. Like actual scientists, students must be able to change their minds as they weigh the scientific evidence behind ideas or approaches. Being able to place new information in context certainly helps.

To more fully understand the scientific method (processes), it is important to investigate a topic in a variety of contexts. With some problems, experimentation may be the way to go.

Formative and portfolio assessment are natural partners for differentiated scientific inquiry. These modern assessment practices are classroom-tested tools for helping teachers and students gather, discover, and evaluate information for themselves. They can also help learners collaborate to generate scientific data and use it to explore topical issues. The next step is coming up with possible solutions to science-related problems.

Knowledge, imagination, and social consciousness matter at least as much as subject matter competency. An important purpose of science instruction is to encourage engagement with democratic processes in a way that prepares students to answer challenging science-related questions.

Although not many teachers *want* to tell their students what to think, many do believe in telling them what is worth thinking about. To participate in making difficult decisions that involve the natural world requires the ability to examine multiple perspectives and simultaneously hold conflicting ideas in one's mind.

A major task in teaching science involves creating classrooms that recognize students as unique thinkers, active investigators, and cooperative problem solvers (Campbell & Fulton, 2003). If scientific literacy is reduced to the solitary acquisition of facts, it should come as no surprise if minds are impoverished.

Education at its best is personal, purposeful, collaborative, and intrinsically motivating. By taking a collaborative path to inquiry, students can directly examine and apply the process skills of science. As active learning teams go about their work, it is possible for group members to communicate more freely, teach one another, and extend their inquiry and discoveries.

The development of scientific skills and understandings depends on tools and products of science—from mathematics and technology to critical thinking and cooperative exploration. Differentiated learning and modern assessment tools are natural partners in connecting active, participatory learning to students' exploration of the natural world.

To experience some of nature's wonder and mystery, students just have to probe the environment around them. As students progress, they will more fully profit from connecting science and related math tools in a way that allows them to explore the situations found in daily life *and* in the larger universe. As Galileo suggested, *mathematics is the language of nature at all levels.*

> *Some important themes pervade science and mathematics, and appear over and over again, whether we are looking at ancient civilization, the human body, or a comet. They transcend disciplinary boundaries and prove fruitful in explanation, in theory, and in design.* —Rutherford and Ahlgren

DISCUSSION POINTS FOR TEACHERS

1. How would you formulate four or five questions about a science/math-related topic that you would like to investigate?
2. For each question you asked, select resources that could be consulted, such as books and other media, places, people, and additional sources of information.
3. If you can, find a teacher who knows more than you do about science or math. Partner with that person and search collaboratively. Record the processes of inquiry. What difficulties were encountered?
4. Reflect on your work with others and your progress toward scientific literacy.

REFERENCES

Abell, S., & Volkmann, M. (2006). *Seamless assessment in science: A guide for elementary and middle school students.* Portsmouth, NH: Heinemann.
Campbell, B., & Fulton, L. (2003). *Science notebooks: Writing about inquiry.* Portsmouth, NH: Heinemann.
Carin, A., Bass, J., & Contant, T. (2005). *Methods for teaching science as inquiry.* Upper Saddle River, NJ: Pearson Education.
Ellis, A. (2010). *Teaching, learning, and assessment: Reflective assessments for elementary classrooms.* Larchmont, NY: Eye On Education.
Etheredge, S., & Rudnitsky, A. (2003). *Introducing students to scientific inquiry: How do we know what we know?* Boston: Allyn & Bacon.
Golden, C. & Katz, L. (2008). *The race between education and technology.* Cambridge, MA: Harvard University Press.
Hassan, R. (2012). *The age of distraction: Reading, writing, and politics in a high-speed networked economy.* New Brunswick, NJ: Transaction Publishers.

Marzano, R. (2010). *Formative assessment & standards-based grading*. Bloomington, IN: Marzano Research Laboratory.

National Council of Teachers of Mathematics (NCTM). (2000). *Principles and standards for school mathematics*. Reston, VA: National Council of Teachers of Mathematics.

National Research Council. (1996). *National science education standards*. Washington, DC: National Academy Press.

National Research Council. (2011). *A Framework for K–12 Science Education Practices, Crosscutting Concepts, and Core Ideas*. Washington, DC: National Academy Press.

Pratt, H. (2012). *The NSTA Reader's Guide to a Framework for K–12 Science Education: Practices, Crosscutting Concepts, and Core Ideas*. Arlington, VA: NSTA.

Rhoton, J., & Bowers, P. (2001). *Professional development leadership and the diverse learner*. Arlington, VA: National Science Teachers Association Press.

Rosenzweig, R. (2011). *Clio Wired: The future of the past in the digital age*. New York, NY: Columbia University Press.

Rutherford, F., & Ahlgren, A. (1990). *Science for all Americans*. New York: Oxford University Press.

Snow, D. (2005). *Classroom strategies for helping at-risk students*. Alexandria, VA: Association for Supervision and Curriculum Development.

Strickland, D., Ganske, K., & Monroe, J. (2002). *Supporting struggling readers and writers: Strategies for classroom intervention 3–6*. Portland, ME: Stenhouse.

Tomlinson, C. (1999). *The differentiated classroom: Responding to the needs of all learners*. Alexandria, VA: Association for Supervision and Curriculum Development.

Tomlinson, C., & Cunningham Edison, C. (2003). *Differentiation in practice: A resource guide for differentiating curriculum*. Alexandria, VA: Association for Supervision and Curriculum Development.

Van De Walle, J., & Lovin, L. (2006). *Teaching student-centered mathematics*. Boston: Allyn & Bacon.

FOUR
Mathematics Instruction

Differentiation, Problem Solving, and Formative Assessment

> *The right question or experience at the right time can move children to peaks in their thinking that result in significant steps forward and real intellectual development.* —Eleanor Duckworth

Today's classrooms are increasingly filled with a diverse cross-section of students. They have varying abilities, learning styles, and just about everything else. Different abilities and interests are evident as students deal with thoughtful questions and mathematical problem solving. There is simply no way that one size can be made to fit all. Differentiated instruction provides flexible possibilities for meeting learners at their level.

In a differentiated classroom, the teacher can do a better job of asking the right question at the right time. As the math standards point out, *all* students can learn to identify and solve authentic mathematical questions and problems (Wortham, 2012).

Here we explore some of the current issues surrounding differentiated math instruction and *in*formative assessment. Some easy-to-adapt math activities are arranged so that you can challenge students who are doing well and support those who are struggling. All of the assessment tools outlined are designed to help teachers understand students' learning profiles so that instruction can be tailored to meet their needs.

Mathematics has always been helpful in revealing hidden patterns for understanding the world. Today, more than ever, students must understand the basic outlines of mathematics to grasp patterns, solve problems, and deal with the ambiguity of a constantly changing world.

The scarcity of math knowledge in the general population is a great concern among policy makers, teachers, and many others. Inadequate preparation has a lot to do with the nation's inability to produce the number of scientists or engineers needed in an innovation-driven global economy. It's not only about producing experts. As far as the general population is concerned, higher levels of mathematical literacy (numeracy) is needed to make informed decisions in a democracy.

Over the last few decades math instruction has achieved a renewed prominence and a lot more attention from educators. The result is that achievement in math has been growing—at least at the elementary and middle-school levels. Still, many American students are not doing well when compared with their international counterparts (Sonnabend, 2009).

The challenge for teachers today is to come up with even more effective approaches for improving mathematical reasoning, problem-solving skills, and positive (confident) attitudes toward mathematics.

CHANGING THE FOCUS IN MATH INSTRUCTION

Mathematics instruction has a lot to do with helping students understand numbers and the relationships between numbers. Other goals include understanding the meaning of arithmetic/mathematical operations, computing fluency, and being able to make reasonable estimates (National Council of Teachers of Mathematics, 2000). The standards also point out that numeracy is to mathematics as literacy is to language.

This chapter goes on to examine

- mathematical reasoning and ways of reaching all students.
- collaborative learning, differentiation, and building new knowledge.
- the NCTM standards and the implications for curriculum and instruction.
- problem-solving strategies and activities for implementing the standards.
- instructional uses of formative, summative, and performance assessment.

Mathematics was the first discipline to come up with the idea of national standards. The math standards suggested many changes in math instruction and made at least some difference in the majority of schools across the country (Whitman, 2006).

The National Council of Teachers of Mathematics (NCTM) recommends teaching basic skills within the context of problem solving. Computation, memorized learning, and routine practice are still in the picture, but the focus is now on reasoning, computational understanding, genuine problems, and connections among math ideas.

Although many teachers don't have a solid background in math, they are all expected to help students master a curriculum that has changed its emphasis. So it's little wonder that so many educators are pointing to professional development as one of the keys to success.

A majority of those who teach math have become familiar with the NCTM standards and take them seriously when they design math lessons.

The standards suggest ending many broad and shallow state standards that force schools to teach dozens of math topics in each grade (Lewin, 2006). (It is often said that math and science instruction are like the Great Salt Lake: twenty-five miles wide, seventy-five miles long, and with an average depth of about fourteen feet.)

Math instruction used to mean attending to the computational skills of arithmetic: addition, subtraction, multiplication, and division, along with whole numbers, fractions, decimals, and percentages. Arithmetic still matters. But today, there is general agreement that a deep understanding of mathematics is much more than facts, figures, and computation (NCTM, 2000).

Traditionally, math instruction did not work for many learners. It produced students who hated math and had little chance of connecting mathematical concepts to anything in their lives—or the world in general. When it comes to traditional math instruction, too many students follow a line from Joan Jett: "Bad attitude, how to get it—and how to keep it."

It all comes down to balance. Not only do students need to know certain basic math facts, but they must also understand how to apply them in realistic situations.

Instruction in mathematics continues to evolve as teachers learn to use the most successful and well-organized teaching methods possible for increasing the participation of all students. Judgments about what to teach and how to teach it has a lot to do with how you assess student work. A blend of formative, summative, and performance assessments can point to student strengths, interests, and needs in a way that helps teachers do a better job of constructing work assignments.

*In*formative assessment techniques enable teachers to adjust instruction quickly and improve students' learning. It also helps teachers attend to those concepts and skills that certain individuals or groups are having difficulty with and encourage the more advanced students to move on to enrichment activities. No matter how it gets done, an important educational goal is accelerating student achievement in mathematics.

A reminder: it is just as bad to say that Jane is bored as it is to say that Johnny can't compute. So have something that is stimulating for students at all levels.

OVERCOMING AN AVERSION TO MATH

Quite a few people have an aversion to mathematics and feel that they would be better off if they could avoid it. As a result, all kinds of misguided ideas stem from policy makers and citizens who don't have a clue when it comes to applying mathematical principles in real life. Innumeracy and illiteracy are flip sides of the same coin.

A good example of innumeracy can be found in the news reports about a legislator in Wisconsin who was against daylight saving time because the extra hour of sunlight would cause fabrics to fade (Paulos, 2001). There are good reasons to oppose changing the clocks, but danger from an extra hour of sunlight isn't one of them.

Typically, students bring widely varying backgrounds to their math lessons, and teachers work hard to accommodate this diversity. On one level, we believe that all students have the potential to learn mathematics. On another level, we have to admit that at least some of them arrive so unprepared that they encounter academic difficulties.

Everyone, from math educators to textbook writers, has been working hard to develop creative and innovative ways to meet the mathematical needs of all students.

Students with attention deficit problems, memory problems, motor disabilities, visual problems, and auditory difficulties require special accommodations in the math classroom to reach their potential. It goes well beyond physical and environmental difficulties. In today's diverse classrooms, we often find English-language learners and others who simply need further basic math instruction.

With some students, it is not a question of language proficiency or disability, but a question of motivation and attitude. But whatever the source of difficulty, providing reluctant math learners with a strong mathematics program will be easier if teachers modify instruction, build teamwork skills, and tap into the natural strength of each student (Benjamin, 2003).

It is best to make sure that the most reluctant and the most advanced learners understand what it means to *know* and *do* mathematics in and out of school.

WHAT IS MATHEMATICS?

Many people have their own ideas of what mathematics is. Which of the following views of mathematics is closest to yours? How will your view of mathematics influence how you help students learn?

1. *Mathematics is a method of thinking and asking questions.* How students make math-related plans, organize their thoughts, analyze data, and solve problems is *doing* mathematics. People comfortable with math are

often comfortable with thinking. The *question* is the cornerstone of all investigation. It guides the learner to a variety of sources revealing previously undetected patterns. These undiscovered openings can become sources of new questions that can deepen and enhance learning and inquiry.

2. *Mathematics is a knowledge of patterns and relationships.* Students need to recognize the repetition of math concepts and make connections with ideas they know. These relationships help unify the math curriculum as each new concept is interwoven with former ideas. Students quickly see how a new concept is similar to or different from others already learned. For example, students soon learn how the basic facts of addition and subtraction are interrelated ($4 + 2 = 6$ and $6 - 2 = 4$). They use their observation skills to describe, classify, compare, measure, and solve problems.

3. *Mathematics is a tool.* It is what mathematicians use in their work. It is also used by all of us every day. Students come to understand why they are learning the basic math principles and ideas that the school curriculum involves. Like mathematicians and scientists, they also will use mathematics tools to solve problems. They soon learn that many careers and occupations are involved with the tools of mathematics.

4. *Mathematics is fun (a puzzle).* Anyone who has ever worked on a puzzle or stimulating problem knows what we're talking about when we say mathematics is fun. The stimulating quest for an answer encourages learners to find a solution.

5. *Mathematics is an art, defined by harmony and internal order.* Mathematics needs to be appreciated as an art form where everything is related and interconnected. Art is often thought to be subjective, and by contrast, objective mathematics is often associated with memorized facts and skills. Yet the two are closely related to each other. Because teachers tend to focus on the skills, they may forget that students need to be guided to recognize and appreciate the fundamental organization and consistency as they construct their own understanding of mathematics.

6. *Mathematics is a language, a means of communicating.* It requires being able to use special terms and symbols to represent information. This unique language enhances our ability to communicate across the disciplines of science, technology, statistics, and other subjects. For example, a struggling learner encountering "$3 + 2 = 5$" needs to have the language translated into terms he or she can understand. Language is a window into students' thinking and understanding. Our job as teachers is to make sure students have carefully defined terms and meaningful symbols. Statisticians may use mathematical symbols that seem foreign to some of us, but after taking a statistics class, we too can decipher the mathematical language. It's no different for children. Symbolism, along with visual aids such as charts and graphs, is an effective way of expressing math ideas to

others. Students learn not only to interpret the language of mathematics, but also to *use* that knowledge.

7. *Mathematics is interdisciplinary.* Math works with the big ideas that connect subjects. Mathematics relates to many subjects. Science and technology are the obvious choices. Literature, music, art, social studies, physical education, and just about everything else make use of mathematics in some way.

Reluctant learners claim they're just not interested in mathematics, working in groups, or discussing the ways that math is used every day. The following activities may help students discover what math is all about. The activities presented here have been field tested with students in elementary and middle-school classrooms. All of them have proven relatively interesting and easy to follow.

DIFFERENTIATED ACTIVITIES THAT HELP GROUPS DEFINE MATHEMATICS

1. *Mathematics is a way of thinking and asking questions.*

Math activity: Have students list all the situations outside of school in which their group used math during the past week.

2. *Mathematics is finding out about patterns and relationships.* Students quickly see how a new math idea is similar to or different from others they already know.

Math activity: Encourage an early-grade math group to show how one math combination(like 4 + 2 = 6) is related to another basic fact (like 6 − 4 = 2). In later grades, students learn how the basic facts of multiplication and division are interrelated (4 × 3 = 12 and 12/3 = 4). They use their observation skills to describe, classify, compare, measure, and solve problems.

3. *Mathematics is a tool.* It is what mathematicians use in their work. It is also used by all of us every day. Like mathematicians and scientists, students use mathematics to solve problems.

Math activity: Solve this problem using the tools of mathematics: A man bought a junk car for $50 and sold it for $60. Then, he bought the car back for $70 and sold it again for $80. How much money did he make or lose? Do the problem with your group and explain your reasoning.

4. *Mathematics is fun (a puzzle).* The stimulating quest for an answer encourages students to find an answer.

Math activity: With a partner, play a game of cribbage (a card game in which the object is to form combinations for points). Dominoes is another challenging game to play in groups.

5. *Mathematics is an art, defined by harmony and internal order.* Many students think of math as a confusing set of facts and skills that must be memorized. Instead, mathematics can be appreciated as an art form

where everything is related and interconnected. After students have mastered the basic facts, they can experience the full potential of math discovery.

Math activity: Have a small group of students design a picture, find geometric shapes, label them, decorate them, and add to them.

6. *Math is a language.*

Math activity: Divide the class into small groups of four or five. Have the students brainstorm about what they would like to find out from other class members (favorite hobbies, TV programs, kinds of pets, and so forth). Once a topic is agreed on, have them organize and take a survey of all class members. When the data are gathered and compiled, have groups make a clear, descriptive graph that can be posted in the classroom.

7. *Math is interdisciplinary.* It connects with many subjects, like music, art, literature, science, and creative movement.

Math activity: With a group, design a song using a rhythmic format that can be sung, chanted, or rapped. The lyrics can be written and musical notation added.

COLLABORATIVE MATH INQUIRY

Collaborative inquiry is a way of teaching that builds on group interaction and students' natural curiosity. Inquiry refers to the activities of students in which they develop knowledge and understanding of mathematical ideas. This active process involves students in asking questions, gathering data, observing, analyzing, proposing answers, explaining, predicting, and communicating the results (Stephen, Bowers, Cobb, & Gravemeijer, 2004).

Collaborative inquiry is supported when students have opportunities to describe their own ideas and hear others explain their thoughts, raise questions, and explore various team approaches. Within a small-group setting, students have more opportunities to interact with math content than they do during whole-class discussions.

The role of the classroom teacher is to help students become aware of how to ask questions and how to find evidence. In today's classrooms, teachers are moving from a "telling" model toward "structured group experiences." This involves encouraging students to interact with one another and value social relationships as they become informed investigators.

The challenge for the teacher is to set up group work so that it engages students in meaningful math activities. In the differentiated classroom, every student is challenged to think and work together to solve problems. The next step is making sure that learners feel secure as they go about applying their understandings.

We want all students to be involved in high-quality, engaging mathematics instruction. High expectations should be set for all, with accommodations for those who need them. Students will confidently engage in mathematics tasks, explore evidence, and provide reasoning and proof to support their work.

As active, resourceful problem solvers, students will be flexible as they work in groups with access to technology. Students value mathematics when they work productively and reflectively as they communicate their ideas orally and in writing (NCTM, 2000).

NCTM STANDARDS FOR SCHOOL MATHEMATICS

The standards make suggestions and provide descriptors of the mathematical content and processes that students should learn. They call for a broader scope of mathematics studies, pointing out what should be valued in mathematics instruction. A comprehensive foundation of what students should know and be able to do is provided. The standards also address the understandings, knowledge, and skills required of elementary and middle-school students.

We often hear complaints from teachers that the state content standards are dictating how they should teach. The content standards indicate *what* you are teaching. They do not tell you *how* to go about teaching the content. How you teach the content has more to do with you. Although there are usually state and district requirements, much of what is done in classrooms comes down to the individual teacher.

Concrete manipulatives like geo-pieces, base-ten blocks, Cuisenaire rods, fraction pieces, and even Popsicle sticks get used a lot in the primary grades. Children of all ages are naturally curious, like to make sense of things, and are natural problem solvers.

In the differentiated classroom, students are often given choices of different projects to work on, and they are encouraged to decide the direction of their work. The teacher builds on prior observation (assessment) to steer students toward projects that play to the strengths of individuals, pairs, or clusters of students. Assignments may vary in difficulty, and there is space for intermediate indicators of progress (formative assessment).

The national math standards suggest that we should make sure that all students are provided with the opportunity to learn significant mathematics. The standards include content (addressing what students should learn) and process (addressing aspects of doing mathematics). The content standards describe the foundations of what students should know. The process standards point to problem solving, reasoning and proof, communicating, making connections, and representing data to express ways of using and applying content knowledge.

The goals articulated by the standards are designed to be responsive to accelerated changes in our society, our schools, and our classrooms. Individual teachers can make alterations for students within their classrooms, but the school itself must have a coherent program of mathematics study for students (Zazkis, 2011). The field of mathematics recognizes the fact that no curriculum should be carved in stone; rather, it must be responsive to the lessons of the past, the concerns of the present, and the human possibilities of the future.

THE 2011 MATHEMATICS FRAMEWORK

Since the 1980s, the National Assessment for Educational Progress has been gathering data on students' understanding of mathematical content. The new framework includes these broad areas:

- Number properties and operations
- Measurement
- Geometry
- Data analysis, statistics, and probability
- Algebra

These new areas are intended to provide an organized system to describe important mathematical concepts and skills (National Assessment of Educational Progress, 2011). This is an assessment framework, not a curriculum framework. It describes the basics of math assessment.

IMPLEMENTING THE CURRICULUM STANDARDS

This section of the chapter connects some of the standards to classroom practice by presenting a few sample activities for each standard. The intent is not to prescribe an activity for a unique grade level but to present activities that can be used in many grades.

NUMBER AND NUMBER OPERATIONS STANDARD

Concepts and skills related to numbers are a basic emphasis for all students. Teachers should help learners strengthen their sense of numbers, moving from initial basic counting techniques to a more sophisticated understanding of numbers if they are to make sense of the ways numbers are used in their everyday world. Our number system has been developing for hundreds of years. The modern system we use today had many contributions from numerous countries and cultures (Reys, Lindquist, Lamdin, Smith, & Suydam, 2003).

There are four important features of the number system:

1. *Place value*. The position of a numeral represents its value; for example, the numbers 21, 132, and 213 represent different ways of thinking about the value of the number 2. In the first case, 2 represents two tens, or 20, the second 2 represents two ones, or 2, and in the third case 2 represents two hundreds, or 200.

2. *Base of ten*. Base in the number system means a collection. In our number system, ten is the value that determines a new collection. Our number system has ten numerals: 0, 1, 2, 3, 4, 5, 6, 7, 8, and 9. This collection is called a *base-ten system*.

3. *Use of zero*. Unlike other number systems, our system has a symbol for zero. Encourage students to think about the Roman numeral system. The reason it is so cumbersome to use today is that it has no zero.

4. *Additive property*. Our number system has a specific way of naming numbers. For example, the number 321 names the number 300 + 20 + 1.

Place value is one of the most important concepts in elementary and middle school. Solving problems that involve computation includes understanding and expressing multidigit numbers. Yet knowing when to exchange groups of ones for tens, or what to do with a zero in the hundredths place when subtracting, for example, confuses many students who then struggle with the step-by-step subtraction problem. Students are helped by solving real-world problems with hands-on materials such as counters, base-ten blocks, and place value charts. Students must create meaning for themselves by using manipulatives (Kilpatrick, Swafford, & Findell, 2001).

The following place value activities are designed to get learners actively involved.

Grouping by Tens or Trading

Students need experiences in counting many objects, trading for groups of tens, hundreds, and thousands—and talking together about their findings. Students need many models. Bean sticks and base-ten blocks are two models widely used by teachers. But students also need piles of materials (rice, beans, straws, counters, and Unifix cubes) to practice counting, grouping, and trading.

Ask students to group by tens as they work. This makes the task of counting easier for students; counting by tens also helps students check errors in their counting. But most important, sorting by tens shows students how large numbers of objects can be organized. Some common errors related to place value include not regrouping when necessary or regrouping in the wrong place (Kamii, 2000).

Trading Rules

The base-ten system works by trading ten ones for one ten, or the reverse, trading one ten for ten ones, ten tens for one hundred, ten hundreds for one thousand, and so on. Base-ten blocks are a great ready-made model in teaching this principle. Encourage students to make their own model. Building models with Popsicle sticks and lima beans works equally well. Or, if teachers wish to have students use construction paper and scissors, students can make their base-ten models by cutting out small squares of paper and pasting them on a ten strip to form a ten. Then, after completing ten tens, paste the ten strips together to make a hundred, and then paste the hundreds together to form a thousand. It is time-consuming work but is well worth the effort.

Proportional models such as base-ten blocks, bean sticks, and ten strips provide physical representation. In all the examples just mentioned, the material for ten is ten times the size of the unit; the hundred is ten times the size of the ten; the thousand is ten times the size of the hundred; and so on. Metric measurement provides another proportional model. Meter stick, decimeter rods, and centimeter cubes can be used to model any three-digit number. Nonproportional models such as money do not exhibit a size relationship but present a practical, real-life model. Because both types of models are important and should be used, we recommend starting students with proportional models as they are more concrete and help learners to understand the relationships more clearly.

Teaching Place Value

It is important that students think of numbers in many ways. A good place to start is to pass out a base-ten mat with the words *ones*, *tens*, and *hundreds*. Also, pass out base-ten blocks to each of the students (units, longs, flats). The units represent ones, longs represent tens, and flats represent hundreds. Now, have the students build the number they hear. If, for example, the teacher says the number 42, the students take four long rods (tens) and place them on the tens column of their mat, and two units, placing them in the ones column. Encourage students to test their skill in a small group by thinking of a number, verbalizing it, and then checking other students' mats.

FRACTIONS

Fraction concepts are among the most complicated and important mathematical ideas that students encounter. Perhaps because of their complexity, fractions are also among the least understood by students. Some of the difficulties may arise from the different ways of representing fractions: spoken symbols, written symbols, manipulative materials, pictures, and real-world situations. It is difficult for struggling students to make sense of these different ways of representing fractions and connecting them in meaningful ways. Learners need many chances to work with concrete materials, observe and talk about fractional parts, and relate their experiences to science and mathematical notation. Three meanings of fractions, part-whole, quotient, and ratio are found in most elementary and middle-school programs.

Part-Whole Fraction Model

Most fraction ideas are based on the part-whole fraction meaning. The part-whole meaning of a fraction such as 3/5 indicates that a whole has been divided into five equal parts and that three of those parts are being used. The fraction may be shown with a model:
[///////] [///////] [///////] [ ] [ ]

Fraction as a Quotient

The fraction 3/5 may also be looked at as a quotient: 3 ÷ 5. This view also comes from dividing something. Imagine you had three big cookies. You want to divide the three cookies among five friends, or 3 ÷ 5. How much would each of your friends get? Each person gets 1/5, 1/5, 1/5, or 3/5.

Fraction as a Ratio

The fraction 3/5 may also represent a ratio, such as there being three boys for every five girls.

Fraction as a Region

The region is the most concrete form of understanding a fraction. It is easily handled by students. The region is the whole, and the parts are congruent (the same size and shape). The region may be any shape, such as a circle, square, or triangle. A variety of shapes may be used so that students do not think that a fraction is always "part of a pizza."

Fraction as a Length

Any unit can be partitioned into fractional parts. A number line is a good example. Oftentimes teachers use manipulatives such as fraction bars; one helpful activity along these lines is to have students make a fraction kit.

Create a Fraction Kit

This introductory activity introduces fractions to students. Fractions are presented as parts of a whole.

Materials: Each student needs seven different 3" × 18" strips of colored construction paper, a pair of scissors, and an envelope in which to put his or her set of fraction pieces labeled as follows: 1, 1/2, 1/3, 1/4, 1/8, 1/12, 1/16.

Directions: Direct students to cut and label the strips as follows.

1. Have students select a colored strip. Emphasize that this strip represents one whole, and have students label the strip 1/1 or 1.
2. Ask students to choose another color, fold the strip in half, cut it, and then label each piece 1/2. Talk about what 1/2 means (1/2 means one piece out of two total pieces).
3. Have students select another color, and have them fold the strip and cut it into four pieces, labeling each piece 1/4. Again, discuss what 1/4 means (one piece out of four total pieces; compare the four pieces with the whole).
4. Have students fold, cut, and label a fourth colored strip into eighths, a fifth strip into twelfths, and a sixth strip into sixteenths.

Now each student has a fraction kit. Encourage students to compare the sizes of the pieces and talk together about what they discover. For example, students can easily observe that the fractional piece for 1/16 is smaller than the piece marked 1/4. This is a good time to introduce equivalent fractions. "How many 1/16 pieces would it take to equal 1/4? What other fractional pieces would equal 1/4?" Explaining equivalence with a fraction kit makes fractions more meaningful (Burns, 2001).

Evaluation, Completion, and/or Follow-up

This follow-up section contains activities that engage students in the use of the fraction kit.

Activity 1—Fraction Cover-Up

Have students work in small groups. Have each student start with the 1 strip. Using the pieces from the fraction kit, challenge students to be the first to cover the whole strip completely. Build a cube and put a different fraction on each side. The game rules are as follows: Have students take turns rolling the cube labeled with fractions. The fraction that is shown when the cube is rolled tells the students the size of the piece to place on the strip. When getting close to the end, students must roll exactly the fraction that is needed.

Activity 2—Fraction Equivalence Game

This game gives students opportunities to work with equivalent fractions. Each player starts with the 1 strip covered with two 1/2 fraction pieces. The challenge is to be the first to remove the strips completely. Encourage students to follow these rules. Students take turns rolling the fraction cube. A student has three options on each turn: to remove a piece (only if he or she has a piece indicated by the fraction on the cube), to exchange any of the pieces left for equivalent pieces, or to do nothing and pass the cube to the next player. A student may not remove a piece and trade in the same turn but can choose to do one or the other.

MEASUREMENT STANDARD

Concepts and skills in the measurement standard deal with making comparisons between what is being measured and a standard unit of measurement. Students acquire measuring skills through firsthand experiences. It is important to remind students that measurement is never exact; even the most careful measurements are approximations. Students need to learn to make estimates when measuring.

Measurement tools and skills have many uses in everyday life. Being able to measure connects mathematics to the real-world environment. Being able to use the tools of measurement such as rulers, measuring cups, scales, thermometers, meter sticks, and so on—and to estimate with these tools—is an essential skill for students to develop.

Instruction in measurement should progress through these attributes of measurement: length, weight/mass, volume/capacity, time, temperature, and area. Within each of these areas, students need to begin making comparisons with standard and nonstandard units. In the upper grades, using measurement tools to measure can be emphasized more.

Sample Measurement Activity: Body Comparisons

Students need direct, concrete experiences when interacting with mathematical ideas. The following activities are designed to clarify many commonly held incorrect ideas.

Finding the Ratio of Your Height to Your Head

How many times do you think a piece of string equal to your height would wrap around your head? Many students have a mental picture of their body, and they make a guess relying on that perception. Have students make an estimate, and then have them verify it for themselves. Few make an accurate guess based on their perceptions.

Comparing Height with Circumference

Have students imagine a soft drink can. Then have them think about taking a string and wrapping it around the can to measure its circumference. Have students guess whether they think the circumference is longer, shorter, or about the same height as the can. Encourage students to estimate how high the circumference measure will reach. Then, have the students try it.

Like the previous activity, many students guess incorrectly. The common misperception is that the string will be about the same length as the height of the can. There is a feeling of surprise or mental confusion when they discover that the circumference is about three times the height of the can. Struggling students feel more confident when they see fellow classmates searching for a correct answer. Repeat the experiment with other cylindrical containers. Have students record their predictions and come up with a conclusion (Burns, 2001).

Group activity: Estimate, measure, and compare your shoes.

Materials: Unifix cubes, shoes.

Procedures: Estimate how many Unifix cubes would fit in a shoe. Students will write their estimates. They choose a volunteer from their group to take off his or her shoe. Then students are instructed to estimate how many Unifix cubes would fit in their shoe. When finished with the estimate, have students actually measure the shoe using Unifix cubes. Students record the measurement. Pass the shoe to the next group; they also estimate and then record the actual measurement. Continue passing the shoes around the class until students have recorded estimates and actual measurements of the shoes from each of the groups.

Evaluation: Instruct students to compare the shoes. Have students explain what attribute of measurement they used. Encourage students to think of another way to measure the shoes. Explain how it might be more accurate (Battista, 2002). Struggling students are actively engaged in estimating and measuring one another's shoes.

PROBLEM-SOLVING STANDARD

Problem solving has been central to elementary mathematics for nearly two decades. Problem solving refers to engaging in a task where the solution is not known. George Polya (1957), a well-known mathematician, devised a four-step scheme for solving problems: understand the problem, create a plan or strategy, follow through with the approach selected, and check back. Does it make sense?

Problems are teaching tools that can be used for different purposes. The solutions are never routine, and there is usually no right answer because of the multitude of possibilities. Strategies include guessing and checking, making a chart or table, drawing a picture, acting out the problem, working backward, creating a simpler problem, looking for patterns, using an equation, using logic, asking someone for help, making an organized list, using a computer simulation, or coming up with your own idea.

Teachers should model the problem-solving strategies needed for thinking about mathematics content or responding to particular math problems. Modeling might include the thinking that goes into selecting what strategy to use, deciding what options are possible, and checking on their progress as they go along. Reluctant learners can catch on quickly if guided through this process. Following are a few problem-solving activities.

Present Interesting Problems

Present a problem to the class. Have students draw pictures of what the problem is about, act out the problem, or have one student read the problem, leaving out the numbers. Once students begin to visualize what the problem is about, they have much less difficulty solving it. Students should work in small groups when arriving at strategies and when solving the problem. Students should write how they solved it and discuss and check their answers with other groups.

The following is a sample problem to present to the class. This is a fun problem for struggling students if they can draw a picture of the animals and think about what the problem is asking.

Solve This Problem

One day Farmer Bill was counting his pigs and chickens. He noticed they had 60 legs and there were 22 animals in all. How many of each kind of animal did he have?

Record your strategy below:

Solve the problem another way:

The standards used were:

Teaching Basic Facts

When students are learning about the operations of addition and subtraction, it is helpful for them to make connections between these processes and the world around them. Story problems help them see the actions of joining and separating. Using manipulatives and sample word problems gives students experiences in joining sets and figuring the differences between them. By pretending and using concrete materials, learning becomes more meaningful. Tell stories in which the learners pretend to be animals or things. Representing ideas and connecting them to mathematics are the bases for understanding. Representations make mathematics more concrete. A typical elementary classroom has several sets of manipulative materials to improve computational skills and make learning more enjoyable.

Base-ten blocks will be used in these activities to represent the sequence of moving from concrete manipulations to the abstract algorithms. Students need many chances to become familiar with the blocks, discovering the vocabulary (ones 5 units, tens 5 longs, hundreds 5 flats), and the relationships among the pieces. The following activities will explore trading relationships in addition, subtraction, multiplication, and division.

The Banker's Game (Simple Addition)

In this activity, small groups of students will be involved in representing tens. The game works best dividing the class into small groups (four or five players and one banker). Each player begins with a playing board divided into units, longs, and flats. Before beginning, the teacher should explain the use of the board. Any blocks the student receives should be placed on the board in the column that has the same shape at the top. A student begins the game by rolling a die and asking the banker for the number rolled in *units*. They are then placed in the units column on the student's board. Each student is in charge of checking his or her board to decide whether a trade is possible. The trading rule states that no player may have more than nine objects in any column at the end of his or her turn. If the player has more than nine, he or she must gather them together, go to the banker, and make a trade (for example, ten units for one long). Play does not proceed to the next player until all the trades have been made. The winner is the first player to earn five tens. This game can be modified by using two dice and increasing the winning amount.

The Take Away Game (Subtraction)

This game is simply the reverse of the Banker's Game. The emphasis here is on representing the regrouping of tens. Players must give back in units to the bank whatever is rolled on the die. To begin, all players place the same number of blocks on their boards. Exchanges must be made with the banker. Rules quickly are made by the students (for example, when rolling a six, a player may hand the banker a long and ask for four units back). It is helpful for students to explain their reasoning to one another. The winner is the first to have an empty playing board. Students should decide in their group beforehand whether an exact roll is necessary to go out or not.

Teaching Division with Understanding

Base-ten blocks bring understanding to an often complex algorithmic process. The following activity is a good place to start when introducing and representing division.

Directions:

1. Using base-ten blocks, have students show 393 with flats, rods, and units.
2. Have the students divide the blocks into three equal piles.
3. Slowly ask students to explain what they did: how many flats in each pile, how many rods, how many units?
4. Give students several more problems. Some examples: Start with 435 and divide into three piles. Encourage students to explain how many flats, rods, and units they found at the end of all their exchanges. In this problem, one flat will have to be exchanged for ten rods (tens), and then the rods divided into three groups. One rod remains. Next, students will have to exchange the one rod for ten units and then divide the units into three groups. No units are left in this problem. Continue doing more verbal problems, pausing and letting students explain how they solved them. What exchanges were made? It is helpful to have students work together trying to explain their reasoning, correcting each other, and asking questions (Burns, 1988).
5. After many problems, perhaps in the next class session, explain to the students that they're now ready to record their work on paper, still using the blocks.

    a. The teacher then shows two ways to write the problem: 435 × 3 and 3/435.
    b. Then the teacher asks the students three questions and waits until all students have finished with each question.

    Question 1: How many 100s in each group? (Students go to their record sheet above the division symbol of the problem. They answer one flat, so they record 1 on their sheet).
    Question 2: How many in all? Students check how many cubes are represented; they answer three hundred, and so they record 300 on their sheet.
    Question 3: How many are left? Students return to the problem and subtract. 435 − 300 = 135.

6. Now, the problem continues with the tens and then the ones. Again, students start over, answering the three questions each time (Burns, 1988).

7. For advanced students, this seems like an elaborate way of doing division. By using manipulatives and teaching with understanding, beginning division makes sense to elementary students. Teachers can introduce shortcuts later to make more advanced division easier and faster.

Students learn best when they are actively engaged in meaningful mathematics tasks using hands-on materials. Such a mathematics classroom encourages students' thinking, risk taking, and communicating with peers and adults about everyday experiences.

Sample Activities

In an effort to link the mathematics standards to classroom practice, a few sample activities are presented. The intent is not to prescribe an activity for a unique grade level, but to present activities that could be modified and used in many grades.

Estimate and Compare

Objectives: In grades K–4, the curriculum includes estimation so that students can

- explore estimation strategies.
- recognize when an estimate is appropriate.
- determine the reasonableness of results.
- apply estimation in working with quantities, measurement, computation, and problem solving.

Math and science instruction in the primary grades tries to make classifying and using numerals essential parts of classroom experience. Children need many opportunities to identify quantities and see relationships between objects. Students count and write numerals.

When developing beginning concepts, students need to manipulate concrete materials and relate numbers to problem situations (Cavanagh, Dacey, Findell, Greenes, Sheffield, & Small, 2004). They benefit by talking, writing, and hearing what others think. In the following activity, students are actively involved in estimating, manipulating objects, counting, verbalizing, writing, and comparing.

Directions:

1. Divide students into small groups (two or three students). Place a similar group of color-coded objects in a container for each group. Pass out recording sheets divided into partitions with the color of the container in each box.

2. Have young students examine the container on their desks, estimate how many objects are present, discuss with their group, and write their guess next to the color on the sheet.
3. Next, have the group count the objects and write the number they counted next to the first number. Instruct the students to circle the greater number.
4. Switch cans or move to the next station and repeat the process. A variety of objects (small plastic cats, marbles, paper clips, colored shells, etc.) adds interest and is a real motivator.

Adding and Subtracting in Everyday Situations

Objectives: In the early grades, the mathematics curriculum should include concepts of addition and subtraction of whole numbers so that students can

- develop meaning for the operations by modeling and discussing a rich variety of problem situations, and
- relate the mathematical language and symbolism of operations to problem situations and informal language.

When students are learning about the operations of addition and subtraction, it's helpful for them to make connections between these processes and the world around them. Story problems using ideas from science help them see the actions of joining and separating. Using manipulatives and sample word problems gives them experiences in joining sets and figuring the differences between them. By pretending and using concrete materials, learning becomes more meaningful.

Directions:

1. Divide students into small groups (two or three students).
2. Tell stories in which the learners can pretend to be animals, plants, other students, or even space creatures.
3. Telling stories is enhanced by having students use Unifix cubes or other manipulatives to represent the people, objects, or animals in the oral problems.
4. Have students work on construction paper or prepare counting boards on which trees, oceans, trails, houses, space stations, and other things have been drawn.

NEW IDEAS ON TEACHING, LEARNING, AND ASSESSMENT

There is general agreement that a constructive, active view of learning must be reflected in the way that math and science are taught (Van De Walle, 2004). Classroom mathematics experiences should stimulate students, build on past understandings, and enable students to explore their own ideas. This means that students have many chances to interpret math ideas and construct understandings for themselves.

To more fully understand the subject, students need to be involved in mathematical problem-solving investigations and projects that engage thinking and reasoning. Working with materials in a group situation helps reinforce thinking. Students talk together, present their understandings, and try to make sense of the task. Students reflect on and evaluate their work.

Some of the newest methods for teaching mathematics in active small-group situations include having students write about how they solved problems, keep daily logs or journals, and express attitudes through creative endeavors such as a building or artwork (Whitin & Whitin, 2000).

Active engagement with mathematics is important at all grade levels. At the primary level, it is particularly important to provide children with room for physical activity in a classroom math environment that encourages active play with others *and* space for quiet or solitary activity.

With the renewed emphasis on thinking, communicating, and making connections among topics, students are more in control of their learning. With collaborative inquiry, students have many experiences with manipulatives, calculators, computers, and real-world applications.

There are good reasons why today's classrooms tend to provide more opportunities to make connections and work with peers on interesting problems. The ability to express basic math understandings, estimate confidently, and check the reasonableness of their estimates is part of what it means to be literate, numerate, and employable.

Whether it's making sense of newspaper graphs, identifying the dangers of global warming, or reading schedules at work, mathematics has real meaning in our lives. The same might be said for using the calculator, working with paper and pencil, or doing mental mathematics. Students must master the basic facts of arithmetic before they can harness the full power of mathematics.

Unfortunately, simply learning to do algorithms (the step-by-step procedures used to compute with numbers) will not ensure success with problems that demand reasoning ability. The good news is that the curriculum is changing to make mathematics more interactive and relevant to what students need to know in order to meet current changing intellectual and societal demands. And it is doing this without dropping the underlying structure of mathematics.

Teachers have found that the more opportunities students have to participate with others, the more likely they are to learn to do mathematics in knowledgeable and meaningful ways. Quite simply, students learn more if they have opportunities to describe their own ideas, listen to others, and cooperatively solve problems. All collaborative or cooperative learning structures are designed to increase student participation in learning, while building on the twin incentives of shared group goals and individual accountability.

IDEAS FOR DIFFERENTIATING MATH INSTRUCTION

- Introduce math ideas in real-world settings.
- Teach an understanding of the math operations (adding, subtracting, multiplying, dividing) by arousing students' natural curiosity.
- Pay attention to students' multiple learning styles and competencies.
- Integrate ideas with the mathematics standards.
- Plan exciting lessons that can be geared up and down.
- Arrange textbook materials to accommodate learners' interests.
- Allow students to explore or go over materials before they use them.
- Use the Internet to access ideas and lesson plans for teaching mathematics.

Remember, peer support helps students feel more confident and willing to make mistakes that go hand in hand with serious inquiry. Student learning teams are a powerful way to approach mathematics instruction in the differentiated classroom. One of the teacher's roles is challenging some and offering assistance to others.

In a world filled with the products of mathematical inquiry, knowing about this subject is more important than ever. Even at the elementary-school level, it is a problem if students don't have a clue about how math impacts their day-to-day lives (Boaler, 2008). Being naive or afraid of math and uninformed about science can be a real problem in school, in the workplace, and in a democratic society.

If too many people lack the understanding to notice, it is easier for someone to distort the math, the statistics, and the science to fit their ideology. Global warming and energy exploration are just two past examples of setting the policy and then searching for some thread of research with the numbers to support it. Obviously, the research should be broad-based and considered before policy decisions are made.

SUMMARY AND CONCLUSION

The best path to mathematical competency involves questioning, investigations, problems, and collaborative activities that are interesting for all students. When students simply memorize concepts and factual material, they find it hard to use what they have learned in new situations.

Learners who are taught math in a passive way are less likely to use it in critical thinking, sense making, or active real-world problem solving

(Murray, 2008). Those who are good at mathematics know that they have to memorize only a limited number of basic methods; the rest is left to an understanding of math concepts and active problem solving.

Mathematical problem solving, collaborative learning, and deductive reasoning are central concerns of today's math curriculum. The best instructional assessment tools for such techniques combine elements of formative, summative, and performance assessment. This approach matches views of learning that recognize that each student has to construct his or her own understanding.

Learning math is much more than absorbing concepts transmitted by the teacher or a textbook. It requires making good use of incoming information and building on existing knowledge.

Self and peer assessment along the learning path certainly helps students achieve academic success. As far as teachers are concerned, in today's fast-paced math lessons, students have to be able to make quick decisions. And they have to do this in circumstances where they do not have all the information. So teachers have to make sure that they understand each student (on many levels) so that they can fill in the gaps.

As teachers go about matching math instruction to the readiness, interests, and talents of all students, the result is likely to be the development of a natural sense of community in the classroom. Being part of a learning team can generate an invitation to imagine, experiment, and explore.

Whether it is the teacher or the student, being able to ask and answer thoughtful real-world questions matters. The processes involved generate confidence and amplify the ability to understand and apply mathematics. The ultimate goal of math instruction: giving students a fascination with mathematics and an appreciation for its power and beauty—while helping them become mathematically empowered.

Knowing is not enough, we must apply.
Willing is not enough, we must do. —Goethe

DISCUSSION POINTS FOR TEACHERS

1. What is a real-world experience that you could use to engage students in a discussion about understanding math operations (adding, subtracting, multiplying, dividing)?
2. List the mistakes that could be made as a result of not understanding math.
3. Design a question or activity that focuses on estimation and problem solving.
4. List some areas of professional development and growth that are important to you. What changes and steps have to be taken to make this happen?

5. How would you focus on helping students make sense of math and see the subject in a more positive light?

REFERENCES

Battista, M. T. (2002). Learning in an inquiry-based classroom. In J. Sowder & B. Schappelle (Eds.), *Lessons learned from research* (pp. 75–84). Reston, VA: National Council of Teachers of Mathematics.

Benjamin, A. (2003). *Differentiated instruction: A guide for elementary school teachers.* Larchmont, NY: Eye on Education.

Boaler, J. (2008). *What's math got to do with it? Helping children learn to love their least favorite subject—and why it's important for America.* New York, NY: Viking.

Burns, M. (1988). *Mathematics with manipulatives* [motion picture]. (Available from Cuisenaire Company of America, White Plains, NY).

Burns, M. (2001). *About teaching mathematics: A K–8 resource.* White Plains, NY: Math Solutions Publications.

Cavanagh, M., Dacey, L., Findell, C., Greenes, C., Sheffield, L., & Small, M. (2004). *Navigating through number and operations in prekindergarten–grade 2.* Reston, VA: National Council of Teachers of Mathematics.

Duckworth, E. (2006). *The having of wonderful ideas: And other essays on teaching and learning* (3rd ed.). New York, NY: Teachers College Press.

John, D. (2012). *Goethe, Faust: German intellectual stagings.* Toronto, Ontario, Canada: University of Toronto Press.

Kamii, C. (2000). *Young children reinvent arithmetic: Implications of Piaget's theory.* New York, NY: Teachers College Press.

Kilpatrick, J., Swafford, J., & Findell, B. (Eds.). (2001). *Adding it up: Helping children learn mathematics.* Washington, DC: National Academy Press.

Lewin, T. (2006, November 14). As math scores lag, a new push for the basics. *The New York Times National.*

Murray, M. (2008). *The differentiated math classroom.* Portsmouth, NH: Heinemann.

National Assessment of Educational Progress. (2010). *Mathematics framework for the 2011 National Assessment of Educational Progress.* Washington, DC: U.S. Department of Educational Research and Improvement.

National Council of Teachers of Mathematics (NCTM). (2000). *Principles and standards for school mathematics.* Reston, VA: National Council of Teachers of Mathematics.

Paulos, J. A. (2001). *Innumeracy: Mathematical illiteracy and its consequences.* New York, NY: Hill and Wang.

Polya, G. (1957). *How to solve it* (2nd ed.). Princeton, NJ: Princeton University Press.

Reys, R., Lindquist, M., Lamdin, D., Smith, N., & Suydam, M. (2003). *Helping children learn mathematics.* New York, NY: John Wiley & Sons.

Sonnabend, T. (2009). *Mathematics for teachers: An interactive approach for grade K–8* (4th ed.). Florence, KY: Brooks Cole.

Stephen, M., Bowers, J., Cobb, P., & Gravemeijer, K. (2004). *Supporting students' development of measuring conceptions: Analyzing students' learning in social context.* Reston, VA: National Council of Teachers of Mathematics.

Van De Walle, J. (2004). *Elementary and middle school mathematics: Thinking developmentally* (5th ed.). Boston, MA: Pearson Education.

Whitin, P., & Whitin, D. (2000). *Math is language too: Talking and writing in the mathematics classroom.* Reston, VA: National Council of Teachers of Mathematics; Urbana, IL: National Council of Teachers of English.

Whitman, N. (2006). *Standards-based math activities for K–8 students: Meeting the needs of today's diverse student population.* Lanham, MD: Rowman & Littlefield Education.

Wortham, S. (2012). *Assessment in early childhood education* (6th ed.). Columbus, OH: Merrill Publishing Co.

Zazkis, R. (2011). *Relearning mathematics: A challenge for prospective elementary school teachers*. Charlotte, NC: Information Age Publishing.

FIVE

Lesson Plans for Science and Math

Informative Assessment and Adjusting the Teaching/Learning Process

> *Don't let the instructionally perfect prevent you from reaping the rewards of the instructionally possible.* —W. J. Popham

This chapter is designed to help educational practitioners who want to use modern assessment methods to improve science and math lessons before, *during*, and after instruction. We include suggestions for differentiated lesson plans and *in*formative assessment techniques.

It is our belief that a well-developed lesson requires a plan to guide instruction. A good lesson plan can also provide the teacher with a reservoir of well-reasoned questions, activities, paths for exploration, and alternative assessment techniques.

Formative and performance assessment techniques involve gathering information in a way that informs learning and improves instruction. It is our belief that assessment should focus more on improving learning than on fill-in-the-bubble testing. We also believe that most standardized tests do not address divergent thinking, creativity, or collaborative problem solving in realistic situations.

Putting standards-based, hands-on science and math instruction into practice doesn't start and stop with the teacher. The same can be said of constructing assessments in alignment with a standards-based curriculum. Administrative support (at all levels) is needed to make it happen. Modern instruction and assessment also require learners to take at least some responsibility for developing their own understanding.

Positive results occur when teachers informally assess students during a lesson: tracking performance, spotting trends, and tailoring instruction to meet the needs of all students (Burke, 2010). Also, both students and teachers can profit when lesson plans provide room for making evidence-based decisions about learning as it is actually happening. This approach has been called a *"trans*formative" framework for formative assessment; it has been shown to help teachers teach better and students learn better (Popham, 2008).

There is now general agreement that it makes sense for teachers to plan what they are going to do in a way that allows for ongoing adjustments in instruction, classroom climate, and each student's framework for learning. This approach involves more than redesigning the soapbox and adding "New and Improved" to the label. The contents of the box have been changed.

Whether assessment is before, during, or after a lesson, it helps if teachers have time to share ideas about what they are planning and how related assessments fit in. Individuals respond favorably when colleagues take their ideas seriously and when reflections on their work are commented on in a constructive manner. As it is now, many teachers spend more time planning alone than they do teaching and talking with other teachers.

Finding a way to share ideas and lesson plans can improve the quality and actually cut the time involved in planning. With a little help from their friends, teachers can more rapidly prepare lesson plans in a way that helps keep the focus on the objective or destination. It can also help them do a better job of dealing with the different reasoning and problem-solving routes taken by students (Zembal-Saul, McNeill, & Harshburger, 2012).

It is clear that competency in science and math is an important building block in the foundation of academic development, life experience, and the human imagination. A country's global competitiveness now comes largely from the capacity of its educational system to develop imaginative citizens who can innovate (Estrin, 2008).

DEVELOPING GUIDELINES FOR THOUGHTFUL SCIENCE AND MATH INSTRUCTION

Innovation builds on the creative spirit and practical know-how in a way that allows new things to be done in new ways—and old things in new ways. The ability to engage with change involves more than being creative at a personal level; it involves others. Space has to be left in our lesson plans for serendipitous discoveries.

Lesson plans are patterns and formats for supporting lessons. Some schools use curriculum guides and textbooks as organizing elements for science and math instruction. Both can serve as starting points or guiding principles for lesson planning. New teachers often turn to the teacher's edition of the textbook for help with planning. Although creative adjustments have to be made, suggested lesson plans are often there for immediate use. If your school district doesn't yet have what you need, publishers, libraries, and the Internet can help.

There is no consensus about the "best" format for a lesson plan. Ask five teachers and you will probably get five answers. Go to the Internet and you will get many more.

For practice and lesson preparation, pick two plans that lend themselves to differentiation and do a Venn diagram (two overlapping circles); place the similarities in the center of the overlap, and place the differences on the outside. Share the results with other teachers.

There is no really good reason to stick with one format. However, you should note that the majority of lesson plans contain the following points: objectives, skills emphasized, materials, procedures, and assessment. The questions experienced teachers answered include the following:

1. What are the learners supposed to learn?
2. How will students learn it?
3. How will I know if they have successfully completed it?

The sample lesson plans and assessment strategies presented here follow a differentiated instructional model that has been field tested with student teachers and in-service teachers. They are research based and standards driven. The lessons are arranged so that they can be altered to fit just about any classroom program or science/math curriculum.

The main goal of lesson planning is to help teachers plan and implement long-, medium-, and short-term objectives. The teacher's edition of the textbook may help, but it is no substitute for creative planning on the part of the teachers. In planning lessons, the classroom environment, the materials available, the diversity of the class, the curriculum, and assessment strategies all come into play.

It always helps if students have plenty of practice in applying new skills and knowledge in unique ways. Such a differentiated approach for activities, lesson planning, and informative assessment can help bring focus to a quality science or math concept, lesson, or unit (Gregory & Hammerman, 2008).

A differentiated lesson plan might include

- *Objectives*: The purpose or lesson goal stating what the student should be able to do after the lesson. Consider multiple intelligences and learning profiles, interest, readiness, and multiculturalism.
- *Content standards*: What students should know and be able to do: unifying concepts in science and math, inquiry, life, earth and space, and physical science.

- *Procedures*: The instructional activities and ways of getting students involved in learning the skill being taught. Activate and engage, explain, and apply learning.
- *Materials*: What the student, the learning group, and the teacher need to successfully complete the lesson.
- *Assessment*: How teachers decide whether the students have achieved what the teacher wanted them to learn. Informative assessment is an ongoing process. Use rubrics for self-evaluation. Portfolio entries show work and progress over time.
- *Accommodations*: Ways of adapting content, materials, and assessment methods so that all students are provided with many ways of learning.
- *Evaluation*: The rating of students' performance, group collaboration, success of the lesson, and teacher effectiveness.

We live in a world that science and math have helped make staggeringly complex. And we ignore that fact at our own peril. Getting students comfortable with science/math ideas and related instructional activities is a road to higher levels of education and a thoughtful life.

Teachers may start a lesson by posing a thought-provoking question or choosing a problem for a collaborative group to work on. Sometimes, the teacher puts forward some possibilities and the pair or small group of students decides which one to explore. At times, the students come up with the questions or problems that they would like to explore.

Whatever the approach, it is important to leave room for ideas and questions rather than answers. This way, students will be encouraged to activate their own thinking and consider the thinking of others.

QUALIFIED TEACHERS AND QUALITIES OF THE MIND

When it comes to science and math instruction, the most important resource is having *fully qualified teachers*. They can move students in the right direction, but good teachers alone may not be able to fully close achievement gaps rooted in broader economic and social inequalities. The American public's attitude toward these issues often seems to be, "Even if it's broken, don't fix it." Things are not "fine the way they are."

Collaborative public action is needed to solve many education-related problems. The good news is that classroom teachers can make all the difference in the world when they are given the educational resources needed to thrive: decent facilities, smaller classes, and a rich science/math curriculum.

In today's typical school classroom, the range of academic diversity makes it very difficult for teachers to teach and assess using the same unaltered procedure for everyone.

The traditional direct instructional lesson/testing model doesn't work for many students. For advanced students, it can lead to boredom, especially if they have already mastered the content. When capable students are bored, they tend to get off task or even become disruptive. For struggling students, the traditional model often fails because the skills needed to do the lesson are missing. As a result, the material is frequently misunderstood, and there is no engagement with the lesson. All too often, the end result is disinterest and disorderly behavior (Chapman & King, 2008).

Providing all students with a safe, structured classroom sets the table for learning both appropriate behavior and content. If you give learners a good reason for doing something, they will probably put up with a little drudgery, whatever their academic standing may be. But whether students are doing well in science and math or not, it helps if time and space are set aside for exploration and self-discovery.

Whether it involves observations, evidence, formulas, comparisons, cause-effect relationships, conclusions, or anything else, increased collaboration and participation can deepen students' understanding of academic content. As cognitive science and neuroscience suggest, building on the social nature of learning and exploring the how's and why's of a subject make it possible for students to unravel problems like a puzzle rather than merely memorize facts or processes for no apparent reason (Sousa, 2008).

In terms of practical advice, we used to think that neuroscience had little to offer and that educators should pay closer attention to cognitive science, psychology, and associated concepts such as multiple-intelligence (MI) theory. Others argued that cognitive psychology and MI theory both have a lot to do with brain science.

The brain and the mind affect everything we do at school, so they have always been natural topics of interest. It's just that now, brain research has reached a stage where it has some practical implications for instructional planning. At the very least, neuroscience research can give teachers some ideas about what *not* to do. Look for more in the future.

Howard Gardner builds on research in cognitive science and psychology to suggest five uses of the mind that will matter even more in the future:

- The *disciplinary mind*—mastery of major schools of thought, including science and mathematics.
- The *synthesizing mind*—ability to integrate ideas from different subjects.
- The *creating mind*—capacity to deal with new problems and questions.
- The *respectful mind*—an appreciation of differences among human beings.

- The *ethical mind*—taking on the responsibilities of citizenship and productive work.

Gardner uses this framework to suggest that the world of the future will demand capacities that, until now, have been options. He also points out that standard measures of learning do not adequately address these "five minds of the future." In addition, norm-referenced tests do not do a good job of measuring whether or not the student has actually learned something that he or she can put to use outside the classroom (Gardner, 2006).

TIERED ACTIVITIES AND DIFFERENTIATED APPLICATIONS

Tiered assignments and assessment are different learning tasks and assessments that teachers develop to meet students' needs. When tiered tasks are used with flexible groups, they usually result in a better instructional match between science/math lessons and individual student needs. In addition, student understanding that comes from the use of differentiated activities is also more likely to transfer to other situations (Tomlinson, Brimijoin, & Narvaez, 2008).

Tiered activities can be arranged by the challenge level based on levels of thinking. They can also be tiered by complexity. Complex tiered activities are designed to be used by levels of difficulty: least complex, more complex, most complex. Another way to tier activities is by learning abilities. When you tier activities by learning abilities, you are matching students' ability levels to their learning needs. Accelerated learners as well as those who have difficulty need to be reminded that every student can be successful.

Teachers use tiered activities so that all students can focus on essential understandings and skills, but at different levels of complexity, open-endedness, and ability. By keeping the focus the same but provoking different ways of reaching the destination, each student is appropriately challenged (Tomlinson & Cunningham-Edison, 2003).

Achieving some mastery in several disciplines certainly helps when it comes to integrating ideas from different fields into a coherent whole. The same can be said of bringing together two previously unrelated subjects: it opens all kinds of new horizons. Also, intellectual curiosity and innovative creativity can be generated when two or more fields have been mastered and the framework from one is used to think afresh about the other.

> *We cannot replace curiosity with mechanical memorization and call it knowledge.* —Paulo Freire

MAKING ASSESSMENT AND PLANNING COUNT

Informative assessment can guide instruction in areas where students are having trouble, much like a meaningful homework assignment does. Examining the reasoning behind errors, as well as figuring out correct approaches, can help teachers and students gain a better understanding of science and math.

Whether you call it formative, informative, or transformative assessment, teachers can adapt instruction by *looking at students' ongoing work* and making changes that will immediately benefit students. In addition, learners can use their current work samples to actively organize and adjust their own learning (Stiggins, Chappuis, & Arter, 2012).

A good lesson/assessment plan includes

1. Looking at whether students have understood the concept.
2. Informally assessing students with one or two quick questions.
3. Discovering which students will need alternative instruction.

The teacher, based on his or her judgment and previous experience with the students, "looks" at which students may have grasped the concept. Then the teacher quickly "assesses" them informally, with a question such as, "Do you understand this idea?" *Discovering* requires a bit more explanation.

In a differentiated class, instructional groups will be formed that will be less supervised by the teacher. Using three or four groups in the classroom means that teachers must assume that students can learn from one another. It's much more than looking for the "right" answers; it's debating, revising, and replacing ideas about scientific findings and mathematical operations. Both teachers and students need to be comfortable with a little trial and error to function well within such a collaborative learning and assessment model.

Informative assessment can take a variety of forms in your classroom. It involves helping students answer these questions:

- *What work am I expected to do?* Give students a list of learning outcomes they are responsible for. Show them some examples of strong and weak performances they are expected to create, and decide which one is better and why.
- *What am I good at, and what do I need to improve?* Have students informally assess their strengths and areas needing improvement. Give students a simple quiz to help both the teacher and students understand who needs to work on what. Share the results with students. Underline words or phrases that reflect specific strengths and areas needing improvement. Keep a record of learning outcomes, and have students check off the ones they've completed.

- *What did I accomplish?* Give students feedback on their work, and have them use it to set personal goals. Encourage students to comment on their progress: what changes have they noticed—for instance, what is easy now that used to be difficult? When students use teacher feedback and learn how to assess their work and look at future goals, they become very involved in their own success. Teachers and students collaborate in an ongoing process using assessment information to improve their learning.

In order to demonstrate *in*formative science/math assessment practices, we designed the following differentiated lesson/assessment plan model. It involves objectives, rationale, prerequisite skills, content standards, organization, and procedures. Each lesson includes materials, student involvement, group arrangements, adaptations, methods for differentiating by gearing up (if the lesson is too easy) or gearing down (if the lesson is too hard), and formative assessment strategies.

DIFFERENTIATED LESSON/ASSESSMENT PLAN MODEL

Topic:
  Grade level:
  Objectives: What do you want students to learn?
  Rationale: Why are the concepts/skills important?
  Prerequisite skills/understandings: What background information do students need before starting?
  Content standards: Have you included the national and state standards for your subject area?
  Organization and procedures:

  List the materials needed.
  How are you going to get the students involved?
  Introduction/anticipatory set.
  Lesson-development questions.
  Closure: How will you end the lesson?
  Small-group options.

  Adaptations:

  Gearing up (if the lesson is too easy).
  Gearing down (if the lesson is too hard).

  Formative assessment: Does your assessment provide evidence of learning the objectives? What evidence will you use to determine that what was taught has been learned (observations, products produced, portfolio entries, reflections)?

CREATING EFFECTIVE INFORMATIVE ASSESSMENT

To connect to the full potential of informative assessment, teachers can

1. Clearly share objectives and criteria for success with students.
2. Lead classroom discussions, question sessions, and learning activities.
3. Activate students by having them assess their own work.
4. Provide students with feedback about what they need to improve.
5. Motivate students to be instructional resources for one another.

Make an Action Plan

Teachers can use good questions to put their own action plans in place. Each teacher needs to make a specific plan about what he or she wants to change. Have teachers voice their expectations. Teachers who concentrate on making a small number of changes and really integrating them into practice make more progress. It is important for teachers to identify how they are going to make time for the new strategies listed above. Some teachers may want to revise their action plans. It is important to provide time for teachers to think it through and check to see whether they made progress (Gareis & Grant, 2008).

DIFFERENTIATED LESSON AND INFORMATIVE ASSESSMENT PLAN 1: SUM SLIDE WITH AUSTE SIAURYTE

Topic: Students will use hundreds chart to find the sums.
 Grade levels: 1 and 2
 Objectives:
 What do you want students to learn? Throughout the year, students have mastered the first standard of being able to count up to two hundred.

- Students have to learn how to add and subtract two-digit problems with or without regrouping.
- The purpose of this lesson is to provide students opportunities to engage in hands-on learning by incorporating both concepts and showing them ways they can use the hundreds chart.

Why are the concepts important? This lesson combines core first- and second-grade standards where students are asked to demonstrate their knowledge of number values up to one hundred and solve problems up to two-digit addition. This lesson will integrate and allow students to practice both concepts as well as learn yet another strategy of how a hundreds chart can be used.

What background information do students need before starting? One-to-one correspondence, addition, and the ability to count to one hundred.

Organization and procedures: The teacher will show the hundreds chart and will ask students to count by fives until they reach one hundred (verbal linguistic).

The teacher will point to the numbers as they are saying them orally (visual/spatial). Then students will be asked to skip-count by fives using their own hundreds chart. Students will be shown an example of how to find a sum of 38 + 47 = 85.

At first, students are asked to solve 38 + 47 using conventional methods, and later, students are shown how to solve the same problem using the hundreds chart (see tables 5.1 and 5.2).

Example: 38 + 47 = 85
Start at 38.
Slide down 4 spaces.
Move forward 7 spaces.
You land on space 85.

Students will be given manipulatives and a hundreds board and will be asked to practice five problems using the hundreds chart (kinesthetic, spatial).

Materials: Hundreds chart, a pencil, manipulatives.

Lesson development, questions, and desired product: First students are taken through a process of recognizing that a hundreds chart can be used to solve addition problems.

After modeling a few problems, students will be asked to try to solve a few of their own using manipulatives. After allowing students plenty of time practicing given problems, students will be asked to pick two partners. One partner will be using the hundreds chart, and the other partner will be using the conventional method. The activity will be stopped after the first partner finishes.

The goal of this "competitive" method is to see which technique yields the most accurate and most prompt results.

Then students will be asked to provide pros and cons useful to their own learning and their evaluation about whether or not they found this technique useful.

Content standards addressed in this lesson:

Number sense:

- Students understand and use numbers up to one hundred.

Table 5.1. Sample Problems

24 + 15 =	25 + 27 =	45 + 22 =	57 + 23 =
11 + 17 =	44 + 38 =	68 + 31 =	76 + 13 =
33 + 54 =	49 + 40 =	30 + 43 =	81 + 16 =

Table 5.2. Hundreds Chart

1	2	3	4	5	6	7	8	9	10
11	12	13	14	15	16	17	18	19	20
21	22	23	24	25	26	27	28	29	30
31	32	33	34	35	36	37	38	39	40
41	42	43	44	45	46	47	48	49	50
51	52	53	54	55	56	57	58	59	60
61	62	53	64	65	66	67	68	69	70
71	72	73	74	75	76	77	78	79	80
81	82	83	84	85	86	87	88	89	90
91	92	93	94	95	96	97	98	99	100

- Students demonstrate the meaning of addition and subtraction and use these operations to solve problems.
- Students solve addition and subtraction problems with one- and two-digit numbers.

Algebra and functions:

- Students use number sentences with operational symbols and expressions to solve problems.
- Students write and solve number sentences from problem situations that express relationships involving addition and subtraction.

Specific differentiation: Students will be shown and modeled the activity for a longer duration.

Students who still struggle with one-to-one correspondence and are not able to count to one hundred will be asked to count using the hundreds chart, moving one number at a time.

Students will be asked to skip-count by twos, fives, and tens.

DIFFERENTIATED LESSON AND INFORMATIVE ASSESSMENT PLAN 2: EXPLORING MULTIPLICATION WITH KATRINA FINLEY, MARISSA LAI, AND JENNIFER ZUBIA

Grade level: 3
What do you want students to learn?

- Students will multiply numbers.
- Students will solve problems by using manipulatives.

Science and math standards: Students will calculate and solve problems.

Entry skills: Counting, addition, grouping, multiplication facts.
Science and math content: Investigating the multiplication tables between one and ten.
Organization and procedures:
Materials: Paper, stickers, chalkboard.
Modeling:

1. Ask two students to come to the front of the room.
2. Ask the class, "How many eyes does each person have?"
3. Ask, "How many eyes are there in total?"
4. Have students describe how they got the answer. (2 + 2)
5. Ask, "What is the multiplication way to get the answer?" (2 people times 2 eyes = 4)
6. Repeat the process with three students.

Guided practice:

1. Students will be instructed to fold papers twice: one lengthwise (hot-dog style) and one crosswise (hamburger style).
2. Then they will copy these problems onto coordinating boxes from the board:
    a. 4 × 3
    b. 3 × 4
    c. 2 × 5
    d. 5 × 2
3. Explain to students that the first number of the problem stands for how many groups there are and that the second number is how many students are in each group.
4. In 4 × 3, there are four boxes. Any kind of box or container will do—the basic idea is to divide things into groups. Students are instructed to place the appropriate number of stickers into each box. (They should put three stickers in each box.) The teacher models this on the board.
5. A tiered challenge approach can be used here. All students make a problem box. For beginners, a problem box could display how many groups there are and list how many stickers each box holds. More advanced learners can compare and contrast the different number of stickers for each group. Question: "How did you decide which box a particular sticker fit into?"
6. Evaluate your selections. As a final activity, have students create a problem box in a new and different way.

Independent practice: Students will make up their own problems to solve. The teacher will observe, make suggestions, and help as needed.

Informative assessment: Students will multiply numbers and solve problems. The teacher will assess students by completion of individual/group work.

1. Teachers explain lesson objectives and how students can be successful.
2. Teachers discuss multiplication, ask questions, and describe multiplication activities.
3. Have students go over their own work.
4. Provide individual students with feedback about what they need to improve on.
5. Encourage students to help and be a resource for one another.

Closure: Students will share some of their multiplication problems. Through their examples, the teacher can reemphasize multiplication principles.

Differentiated accommodations: During independent practice, make sure students understand the directions. Go over any vocabulary with them, and work with students on a few problems. If making up the problems is too complex, write out problems for them to work on. Check on their progress periodically.

SCIENCE AND MATH MEASUREMENT—DIFFERENTIATED LESSON AND INFORMATIVE ASSESSMENT PLAN 3: TREE MEASUREMENT BY DOREEN TOOFER

Grade level: 4

Topic: Science/math measurement

What do you want students to learn? This activity is used to help students understand vertical and horizontal measurement of large objects.

Objectives: Students will be able to

1. Demonstrate measurement of the trunk, crown, and height of a tree using vertical and horizontal measurement.
2. Compare their results with those of other groups.
3. Create a graph of their findings for the trunk, crown, and height.

Materials: String, ruler, paper, pencil, meter stick, tree, portfolio.

Standards: Inquiry, life science, science and technology, personal perspectives, and written communication.

Procedures:

- Students will work with a partner and go outside to find a tree to measure.
- Students will measure the tree's trunk, crown, and height as much as possible.

- Have groups compare answers, and then remeasure the tree as needed. Usually it takes several measurements.

Trunk:

1. Measure from the ground to 4-1/2 feet high on the trunk.
2. At that height, measure the trunk's circumference. Use a string to measure around the trunk, and record the length of the string.
3. Round to the nearest inch. Record the number and label it as the circumference.

Crown:

1. Find the tree's five longest branches.
2. Put markers on the ground beneath the tip of the longest branch.
3. Find a branch that is opposite it and mark its tip on the ground.
4. Measure along the ground from the first marker to the second marker.
5. Record the number and label it as the crown.

Height:

1. Have your partner stand at the base of the tree.
2. Back away from the tree, holding your ruler in front of you in a vertical position. Keep your arm straight. Stop when the tree and the ruler appear to be the same size. (Close one eye to help you line it up.)
3. Turn your wrist so that the ruler looks level to the ground and is horizontal. Keep your arm straight.
4. Have your partner walk to the spot that you see as the top of the ruler. Be sure the base of the ruler is kept at the base of the tree.
5. Measure how many feet he or she walked. That is the tree's height. Round to the nearest foot and record your answer as the height.

Follow-up activity:

- Have students make bar graphs using information gathered outside. Have students locate the biggest tree and smallest tree of the same species.
- For the bar graph, students will be given markers and chart paper to create a bar graph from the information they gathered.

Formative assessment: Teachers will assist students in their measurements and provide feedback. Students should be able to correctly write down their measurements and label them. Teachers will go over student worksheets with all their data, making sure that students are measuring length, width, and height correctly. In addition, the bar graph will be a good assessment of their findings and data organization. Students will reflect on their lesson and put their data and measurement results in their portfolio.

VALUES: A MORAL DILEMMA—DIFFERENTIATED LESSON AND INFORMATIVE ASSESSMENT PLAN 4: MEASURING STICKS

Process skills: Observing, inferring, communicating (sharing), and comparing.

Description: Oftentimes, elementary and middle-school students are quick to compare and criticize others. This activity stresses similarities and attempts to play down differences. The method used in this activity is creative drama. Creative dramatics involves children in group interaction. It is especially useful for reaching out to ESL (English as a second language) learners, allowing them to work with other students while developing oral language. Creative dramatics is a drama for the actors themselves—connecting their feelings and attitudes with reading, literature, and other language skills.

In recent years, teachers have become interested in finding ways to bring students' values and moral decisions into their classrooms. Activities drawn from these areas involve and motivate youth partly because they focus on issues that students really care about. Students are particularly stimulated by questions that deal with their own values, such as: Who am I? What do I care about? How am I perceived by others? How might I change? What kinds of things do other people think important?

Values and morality activities can be taken from newspapers, personal experiences, or books. The skills of using language, valuing, recording, gathering data, and sharing ideas are all part of the foundation of the communication goal explored here.

Sample Moral Development Activity: Laura's Dilemma

Laura and her best friend, Vicki, walked into a department store to shop. As they looked around, Vicki saw a bathing suit she really liked and told Laura she wanted to try it on. While Vicki went to the dressing room, Laura continued to shop.

After a short time, Vicki came out of the dressing room fully dressed. She caught Laura's attention and, without a word, turned and walked out of the store. Moments later, the store security officer, the store manager, and the store clerk approached Laura. "That's her, that's one of the girls. I know her friend walked off with a new bathing suit under her clothes," the clerk said. "I think they planned this together."

The security officer asked the manager whether he wanted to follow through on the case. "Absolutely," he insisted. "Shoplifting is costing us a lot." The security officer turned to Laura. "What's the name of the girl you were with?" he asked. Laura looked at him silently. "Come on, now, tell the truth," said the security officer. "If you don't tell us, you'll be aiding the person who committed the crime, and that's a crime, too."

Should Laura tell? Why or why not?

Objectives:

1. Students will describe and become familiar with the issues.
2. Students will take a position on the dilemma.
3. Students will present an argument based on their position.
4. Students will plan their debate strategies with their group.
5. Students will demonstrate the ability to work in groups in an organized and productive manner.
6. Students will actively participate in the debate.

Process skills: Communicating, analyzing, solving problems, collecting data, and reflecting.

Standards: Inquiry, personal perspectives, and written communication.

Procedures:

1. Introduce students to moral reasoning by asking them to think about times when they weren't sure what would be the right thing to do.
2. Students will show their understanding of the issue (dilemma) by discussing, reading it aloud, or acting it out.
3. Students will divide into small groups, making sure that each group has roughly equal numbers on both sides of the issue.
4. Students will discuss the issue within their small group and plan their debate strategies for the group.
5. In small groups, students will prepare a list of reasons that support their group position. For example, students who say "turn Vicki in" would form a group and come up with the best reasons for turning Vicki in, and the students who say "keep quiet" would meet to come up with reasons to support their position. (In a thirty-student class, the teacher might end up with five groups of six students—two groups figuring out the best reasons to tell, and three groups coming up with the best reasons for not telling.)
6. Last, students will conduct their debates for the class, based on their position.
7. A class discussion of the reasons would come at the end. When the discussion is completed, the teacher may wish to share his or her opinion.

Informative assessment: Encourage students to reflect on this activity by putting their ideas in writing. Some suggestions follow. Working in groups, choose one assessment activity:

- Write an article for your class newspaper.

- Write a letter to students in other classes, suggesting issues for debate.
- Make a video of the outstanding debate in your class.
- Reflect on the lesson.
- Put your work in your portfolio.
- Have students provide feedback to other groups and include suggestions.

LIFE SCIENCE—DIFFERENTIATED LESSON AND INFORMATIVE ASSESSMENT PLAN 5: LEAF EXCHANGE

The falling motions of a leaf are very complex. Sometimes the leaf may drift randomly to the right or left as it falls. At other times it may tumble erratically while maintaining a downward course . . . suggesting [its] motion is chaotic.
—I. Peterson

With the dramatically colorful fall season, it seems like an ideal time to set up a leaf exchange with students in other regions of the country. If it's not fall—or if everything stays green all year—the shapes of leaves can also be quite interesting. Students are naturally captivated with gathering, comparing, and preserving leaves. This activity gets students involved in collecting and gathering many different types of leaves; they examine, sort, classify, investigate, and discover patterns.

Leaf exchange is a class-to-class leaf exchange similar to having pen pals. Leaf exchanges get everyone interested and active—from collecting and classifying leaves into a range of sizes, shapes, and textures, to observing similarities and differences in leaves. Students learn to appreciate the value of exchanging data and gain experience in communicating with students from another region of the country. Student awareness is heightened to the wide variety of plants and trees in their own environment. A class map is then set up to track the journeys of the leaves.

Process skills: Gathering, identifying data, communicating, exploring preserving methods, comparing, graphing, and sharing.

Planning group: Members should arrange the classroom and materials.

Description: Communicating at a personal level for elementary and middle-school students can be very rewarding and exciting.

Objectives:

1. Students will collect and gather leaves.
2. Students will choose a leaf exchange partner.
3. Students will sort, classify, and discover patterns.
4. Students will participate in preserving the leaves they gathered.
5. Students will improve their observation skills and increase their awareness of the plants in their environment.

6. Students as leaf pals will learn how their environment compares with those of others.
7. Students will learn to appreciate the value of exchanging data.

Standards: Inquiry, life science, personal social perspectives, and written communication.

Procedures:

1. Introduce students to leaf exchange, a class-to-class leaf exchange similar to pen pals. Explain that they are going to take part as a class exchanging preserved leaves with students in another area of the country.
2. The first step in this project is to gather leaves for the exchange. Have students bring in leaves from their neighborhoods, or take students on a nature walk.
3. Students are to collect at least ten different leaves.
4. When returning to the classroom, focus students' attention on the leaves' colors, shapes, and sizes.
5. Most students will want to identify the leaves. Using reference materials (slides, computer disks, prints, etc.), have students label each leaf.

Methods for preserving the leaves:

1. *Press/dry method* — Place the leaves in an old telephone book, newspaper, or magazine; apply bricks or weights on top (to permanently preserve, use a laminating process).
2. *Quick iron method* — Preheat iron to permanent press setting. Place a thin sheet of cardboard on the ironing board.
   a. Cut two pieces of wax paper that are larger than the leaf to be pressed. Lay one piece of wax paper on top of the cardboard, place the leaf on top of the wax paper, and put the second piece of wax paper on top of the leaf.
   b. Cover the wax paper with a cotton rag, and then press with the iron each part of the leaf for at least twenty seconds.
   c. Remove the rag, cool the leaf for about two minutes, and carefully peel the wax paper from the leaf.
3. *Preserving leaves with glycerin* — You will need these materials: 1.5 liters of water; 750 milliliters of glycerin (available at drugstores); a 500-milliliter measuring cup; newspaper; a shallow pan. You will have enough room in the pan to preserve about seventy leaves. The remaining solution can be saved.
   a. Mix the glycerin and water in the pan.

b. Place the leaves in the solution, making sure that each leaf is completely coated and that the students are wearing aprons and goggles.
c. Soak the leaves in the solution for twenty-four hours.
d. The next day, remove the leaves. Press each one between newspapers for three days or until completely dry.
e. These pressed leaves will be flattened, making them easier to mail.

4. *Lamination*—If teachers have access to laminating equipment, they can preserve leaves for many years.

a. Dry and press leaves using one of the drying methods, making sure leaves are dry.
b. Follow laminating machine directions.
c. Insert the leaves like a flat piece of paper.
d. Trim the lamination film around each leaf.

Before packaging the leaves, have students compose a letter to their leaf partner describing the leaves and why they chose to send them.

Informative assessment: Have students make a wall map charting where their leaves were sent. Research the vegetation of the areas; do a comparison analysis. Put the data into the computer. Have students reflect on the lesson and put their findings in their portfolio. Have students provide feedback to one another. This activity was adapted from M. Shelton's article in *Science and Children*, 1994.

PHYSICAL SCIENCE—DIFFERENTIATED LESSON AND INFORMATIVE ASSESSMENT PLAN 6: EXPLORING SUPPORTS

Description: There are many kinds of structures that can be described in the natural world. This beginning activity attempts to show how different kinds of structures are related. In this activity, children will find out about supports. The skills introduced include experimenting, testing strength and durability, comparing size and weight, recording data, and communicating. Introduce the activity by talking about structures, the classroom, and tables in the room. Generate questions, such as: What makes the ceiling stay where it is? What keeps the table from falling? Students will soon come up with the idea of structural support. The walls of the classroom and the ceiling supports hold up the ceiling, and the legs on the table keep it from falling. Discuss these ideas with the class. Explain that the name we give to these items is "structural support."

Process skills: Measuring, comparing, inferring, ordering by distance, and formulating conclusions.

Planning group: Members should arrange the classroom and materials.

Materials: Give each of the students some items to form a tower (a cardboard box, a tall block of wood, a paper towel roll, for example). Provide them with the following support materials: styrofoam, wood, cartons, slotted cardboard boxes, and so on; supply some clay, sand, and white glue. Include the following art materials: paints, brushes, construction paper, scissors, paste, and felt pens.

Objectives:

1. When presented with a problem of how to support their tower, students will explore with materials.
2. Students will discuss and share their discoveries with other class members after experimenting and trying many different support structures.
3. Students will compare their tower supports with those of other children.
4. Students will test the strength of their tower.
5. Students will modify their support structure by adding a balcony.
6. Children will decorate their towers.
7. Students will present their investigation by answering these questions:

    Describe how your tower and balcony are supported.
    Show how much weight your balcony holds.
    Explain how you made your supports.

Standards: Inquiry, physical science, personal and social perspectives, and written communication.

Procedures:

1. Challenge the students to find a way to make their tower stand up so that it cannot be blown over by a strong wind.
2. Helpful ideas for getting started:

    Glue supports around the base of the tower.
    Fill a box with sand.
    Attach the base to a larger surface.
    Set the tower in sand or clay.

3. After students have determined a way to support their towers, have them share what they found out.
4. Children can compare their solutions and test their towers to see how strong they really are. For example, students may decide to test their tower by having six or more students blow on it at once. Or they could place a fan near their tower to see whether it continues to stand up.
5. Encourage students to experiment further with different supports to make their towers as sturdy as they can be.

6. Have children decorate their towers with the art supplies provided.

Informative assessment: To find out how much they learned about supports, present students with another challenge. Using any of the materials, can you construct a balcony? Then test it by adding weights. How many weights (if any) will your balcony hold? Add more and more weights until it begins to show signs of collapsing. This activity was adapted from Joan Westley's *Constructions*, 1988, p. 22.

DIFFERENTIATED LESSON AND INFORMATIVE ASSESSMENT PLAN 7: INTERDISCIPLINARY BRIDGE BUILDING

This is an interdisciplinary activity that reinforces skills of communication, group process, social studies, language arts, mathematics, science, and technology.

Purpose and objectives: This is an interdisciplinary science and math activity that reinforces skills of communication, group process, social studies, language arts, mathematics, science, and technology.

Standards: Students use the science and math standards of collaborative learning, investigation, experimentation, measurement, and reasoning.

Materials: Lots of newspaper and masking tape; one large, heavy rock; and one cardboard box. Have students bring in stacks of newspaper. You need approximately one foot of newspaper per person. Bridges are a tribute to technological efforts that employ community planning, engineering efficiency, mathematical precision, aesthetics, group effort, and construction expertise.

Procedures:

1. For the first part of this activity, divide students into three groups. Each group will be responsible for investigating one aspect of bridge building.

    Group one: Research—This group is responsible for going to the library and looking up facts about bridges, collecting pictures of kinds of bridges, and bringing back information to be shared with the class.

    Group two: Aesthetics, art, literature—This group must discover songs, books, paintings, artwork, and so on that deal with bridges.

    Group three: Measurement, engineering—This group must discover design techniques, blueprints, angles, and measurements of actual bridge designs. If possible, visit a local bridge to look at the structural design and other aspects. Pictures also help.

2. Each group presents its findings to the class.

The second part of this activity involves actual student bridge construction.

1. Assemble the collected stacks of newspaper, tape, the rock, and the box at the front of the room. Divide the class into groups of four or five students.
2. Each planning group member is instructed to take an even portion of newspaper to his or her group, plus one or two rolls of masking tape. Explain that the group will be responsible for building a stand-alone bridge using only the newspapers and tape. The bridge is to be constructed so that it will support the large rock and so that the box can pass underneath.
3. Each group is given three to five minutes of planning time in which members are allowed to talk and plan together. During the planning time, they are not allowed to touch the newspapers and tape, but they are encouraged to pick up the rock and make estimates of how tall the box is.
4. At the end of the planning time, students are given ten to twelve minutes to build their bridge. During this time, there is no talking among the group members. They may not handle the rock or the box—only the newspapers and tape. (A few more minutes may be necessary to ensure that all groups have a chance of finishing their constructions.)

Informative assessment: Stop all groups after the allotted time. Survey the bridges with the class, and allow each group to try to pass the two tests for its bridge. (Does the bridge support the rock, and does the box fit underneath?) Discuss the design of each bridge and how it compares to the bridges researched earlier.

Feedback—enrichment: As a follow-up activity, have each group measure its bridge and design a blueprint (include angles, length, and width of the bridge) so that another group could build the bridge by following this model.

DIFFERENTIATED LESSON AND INFORMATIVE ASSESSMENT PLAN 8: BUILDING VISUAL MODELS—CONCEPT CIRCLE

Science teachers can make use of a variety of diagrams to help students grasp important concepts. Mapping concept circles demonstrates meaning and develops visual thinking. Have students represent their understanding of science concepts by constructing concept circles following these rules:

1. Let a circle represent any concept (plant, weather, bird, etc.).

2. Print the name of that concept inside the circle.
3. When you want to show that one concept is included within another concept, draw a smaller circle within a larger circle. For example, large circle—planets; smaller circle—Earth.
4. To demonstrate that some elements of one concept are part of another concept, draw partially overlapping circles. Label each. (For example, water contains some minerals.) The relative size of the circles can show the level of specificity for each concept. Bigger circles can be used for more general concepts or used to represent relative amounts.
5. To show two concepts are not related, draw two separate circles that are not connected and label each one. (For example, bryophytes—mosses, without true leaves; tracheophytes—vascular plants with leaves, stems, and roots.)

Objectives:

1. Students will work with a partner.
2. Students will choose a topic and make a concept circle.
3. Students will describe their visual model.

Formative assessment: Students will explain how the concepts are related. Students will write about how two concepts are not related and explain their chart. Students will put their written reports and charts in their portfolios. Have students provide feedback to one another.

INNOVATIVE INTERDISCIPLINARY ACTIVITIES— DIFFERENTIATED LESSON AND INFORMATIVE ASSESSMENT PLAN 9: ACTIVE PLAY IN ART AND SCIENCE

Play is not only important in the development of the intelligence of children, but it also emerges over and over as an important step in invention and discovery. Curiosity, play, and following hunches are particularly important in developing one of the most valuable scientific tools—intuition.

Objectives:

1. Ask students to bring in materials that are cheap, durable, and safe (such as toys, household objects, etc.). With older students, you may want to include hammers, nails, bolts, lumber, and so on.
2. Divide students into groups of five or six. By playing with the assembled objects, have students make discoveries about the sound potential of the objects they have brought in.

Procedures: Using the objects available to their group, students are to design a device that makes sound. Encourage students to use a variety of objects in as many different ways as possible. When individual designs are complete, have students share their ideas with the group.

Informative assessment: The group must pick one design and work on its construction. The important thing during this noisy period of play is to explore the rich realm of possibilities before arriving at one solution. Instruct students to put their construction in their portfolio. Have students write about their sound solution. Encourage students to provide feedback to other groups.

AWARENESS OF THE ENVIRONMENT—DIFFERENTIATED LESSON AND FORMATIVE ASSESSMENT PLAN 10: CREATING A SOUND GARDEN

Objectives: Ask students to imagine what things they could hear in a garden: birds, the sound of the wind, leaves, human noises, and so on. Discuss various ways sound could be generated in a garden, through wind, by walking, or by having sprinklers running, for example. Next, have students brainstorm ideas for a sound garden. Encourage creativity, fun ideas, and original inventions.

Materials: Suggest inexpensive things that will hold up outdoors and will be safe for other children to play with (things that make sounds when walked on, when touched, etc.).

Procedures: Have students draw up a design for their planned construction and then bring ideas and items from home to contribute to the project. As a group, have them plan and construct their sound garden based on the items. Designs may have to be altered as the class progresses on the project, enabling students to see the ongoing development process as ideas progress and are adjusted to fit the materials and needs of construction.

Informative assessment: Students must determine the best way to display their sound structures so that they will be accessible to others, function well, and create the best visual display in the garden. Have students write a step-by-step plan to design their sound garden and put their plan in their portfolio. A sample short portfolio assessment plan follows.

Portfolio Topic:
Teacher:
Date:

1. Topics, questions, procedures, reasoning, or process skill explored:
2. Areas of growth and difficulties in understanding:
3. Areas where the work is unfinished or could be improved:
4. Write three things you liked about the work and one thing you didn't:
5. Assessment of the following areas:

a. Inquiry and problem-solving work:
   b. Reasoning, discovery, and creative thinking:
   c. If you consulted with a partner or a small group, how did the collaboration work out and how might the process be improved?
   d. What did you find out that was strange or new to you?
   e. What would you like to know more about the topic?

DIFFERENTIATED LESSON AND FORMATIVE ASSESSMENT PLAN 11: EXPLORING EARTH'S POLLUTION

Pollution is defined as an undesirable change in the properties of the lithosphere, hydrosphere, atmosphere, or ecosphere that can have deleterious effects on humans and other organisms. A part of the task for students is to decide what an undesirable change is, or what is undesirable to them. Tell the students they are going to classify pollution in their neighborhood and city. The classification will be based on their senses and the different spheres of the earth — lithosphere (Earth's crust), hydrosphere (Earth's water), atmosphere (Earth's gas), and ecosphere (the spheres in which life is formed). Give each student an observation sheet, or have students design one that shows examples of pollution for a week.

Informative assessment: Have students reflect on their observations. Encourage students to provide feedback to one another. Instruct students to put their data and written reflections in their portfolio.

DIFFERENTIATED LESSON AND FORMATIVE ASSESSMENT LESSON 12: EXPERIMENTING WITH THE UNINTENDED CONSEQUENCES OF TECHNOLOGY

Soap Drops Derby

Students will develop an understanding that technological solutions to problems, such as phosphate-containing detergents, have intended benefits and may also have unintended consequences.

Objective: Students apply their knowledge of surface tension. This experiment shows how water acts like a stretchy skin because water molecules are strongly attracted to one another. Students will also be able to watch how soap molecules squeeze between the water molecules, pushing them apart and reducing the water's surface tension.

Background information: Milk, which is mostly water, has surface tension. When the surface of milk is touched with a drop of soap, the surface tension of the milk is reduced at that spot. Since the surface tension of the milk at the soapy spot is much weaker than it is in the rest of the milk, the water molecules elsewhere in the bowl pull water molecules away from the soapy spot. The movement of the food coloring reveals these currents in the milk.

Grouping: Divide the class into flexible groups of four or five students.

Materials: Milk (only whole or 2 percent will work), newspapers, a shallow container, food coloring, dishwashing soap, a saucer or a plastic lid, toothpicks.

Procedures:

1. Take the milk out of the refrigerator half an hour before the experiment starts.
2. Place the dish on the newspaper and pour about half an inch of milk into the dish.
3. Let the milk sit for a minute or two.
4. Near the side of the dish, put one drop of food coloring in the milk. Place a few colored drops in a pattern around the dish. What happened?
5. Pour some dishwashing soap into the plastic lid. Dip the end of the toothpick into the soap, and touch it to the center of the milk. What happened?
6. Dip the toothpick into the soap again, and touch it to a blob of color. What happened?
7. Rub soap over the bottom half of a food coloring bottle. Stand the bottle in the middle of the dish. What happened?
8. The colors can move for about twenty minutes while students continue dipping the toothpick into the soap and touching the colored drops.

Follow-up evaluation: Students will discuss their findings and share their outcomes with other groups.

Formative assessment: Instruct students to reflect on the experiment. Have them describe some of the benefits of detergents and some unintended consequences. Have them research common phosphates, including detergents and other cleaning products. Have students put their written report in their portfolio. Have students provide feedback to other groups with suggestions for future environmental products.

PHYSICS—DIFFERENTIATED LESSON AND FORMATIVE ASSESSMENT LESSON 13: DISCOVERING BERNOULLI'S PRINCIPLE

Science activities often have surprising results. For example, try a simple activity that uses a Ping-Pong ball and a funnel to demonstrate pressure. Show the class a Ping-Pong ball inside a funnel. Set up the problem. Ask how far students think the Ping-Pong ball will go when they blow into the funnel. What happens? Students will soon discover that when they blow into the funnel, the ball doesn't move. They are proving Bernoulli's principle that when air moves faster across the top surface of a material, the pressure of the air pushing down on the top surface is lower than the pressure of the air pushing up on the bottom surface. There are many variations of the "right answer."

Objectives:

- Present the problem to the class.
- Have students guess what is happening to the Ping-Pong ball.
- Encourage students to write about the experiment.

Procedures:

- Have students work with a partner.
- As a class, have them guess how the experiment works.
- Have them record their guesses in their portfolio.
- Have students do the experiment and explain what is happening.

Formative assessment: Have students explain how this activity showed the properties of air. Air has pressure. Air has weight. Air is invisible, but it is real and it takes up space. Anything that has weight pushes or presses against things. Moving air exerts pressure. Students should be able to come up with a reasonable solution. Instruct students to provide feedback to other groups and give suggestions.

THE FINAL ASSESSMENT

The final assessment usually occurs at the end of a unit or topic of study. It is a culminating experience involving several lessons and reflections. The following is a list of criteria for assessing lessons and unit plans:

1. Subject matter standards for your subject need to be listed.
2. Lesson objectives should clearly state what students will learn.
3. A rationale needs to be included explaining why it is important to teach this concept and skill at this time.
4. Prerequisite skills need to be identified.
5. It is important to look at background information before beginning the lesson.
6. Procedures should be well defined and organized.
7. Materials need to be accessible for teaching the lesson.
8. Small-group options and adaptations need to be provided.
9. Techniques for gearing up the lesson if material is too easy and gearing down the lesson if too difficult need to be available to the teacher.
10. Informative assessment is an ongoing piece of a good unit or lesson.

Whatever type of lesson plan and related assessment technique you decide to use, teacher-directed experiences, small-group activities, individual responsibilities, and informative evaluation techniques can all be briefly spelled out in a one- or two-page plan. (Of course, there are always factors to think about that go beyond the plan.)

Figuring out time and place for using the technological products of science and math is part of lesson planning. Does too much use early on threaten original thinking and face-to-face communication? It's an open question. So teachers have to ask themselves: when is technology the best tool for what they want to accomplish—or can paper, math manipulatives, or real paint do the job just as well or better?

The research on the effectiveness of science and math software is not all that encouraging (Domine, 2009). As far as the teacher is concerned, the instructional payoff from either technology or lesson planning has to be worth the effort. Less is often more because asking for too much paperwork or imposing the use of digital devices can result in teachers mechanically meeting the requirements—or avoiding the process altogether.

IMPROVING THE QUALITY OF CLASSROOM EXPERIENCES

The National Research Council's recent *Framework for K–12 Science Education* provides up-to-date ideas and procedures for instruction. It goes on to explain the role of core ideas, cross-cutting themes, and actual scientific practice in science learning.

The standards suggest that teachers use formative and performance assessment techniques to more fully understand students' individual talents, regardless of cultural background or learning differences.

In today's differentiated science and math classroom, assessment is more than teaching a chapter or unit and giving a test at the end (Hibbard, 2008). There needs to be intermediate checks (formative assessment) of understanding if learning is going to be maximized.

When it comes to quality of classroom experiences, it certainly helps if teachers can design their own formative assessments and provide students with frequent feedback about their work. In such classrooms, teachers interact frequently with students on a daily basis.

As far as lesson planning is concerned, teachers must take into account how assessment can amplify students' opportunities for understanding how the subject being studied relates to the world outside of school.

As differentiation is added to the instructional and assessment mix, the result is a formula that has the possibility of providing *everyone* in the classroom with powerful intellectual tools for imagining unique applications and new approaches.

Providing students with situations where they make discoveries through their investigations often sparks new ideas and scientific ways of thinking. In the formative assessment-centered classroom, students play an active role in their own learning and support the learning of others (Keeley, 2008).

The content standards for science and mathematics have many good ideas and suggestions for teaching. In science, for example, it has a lot to do with helping students acquire scientific knowledge by thinking critically, inquiring collaboratively, and using scientific processes to achieve knowledge about the world. In math, it means making sure that students get a sense of the subject and learn to solve problems through mathematical reasoning.

Even in an innovation-driven rapidly changing world, it isn't all about personal creativity. Students are still taught to recognize, respect, and critically examine ideas and discoveries of major figures and thinkers in whatever subject they are studying.

Neither collaborative inquiry nor problem solving rules out teaching for content. In science, inquiry frequently comes into contact with basic scientific principles. In math, interpretation and discovery don't rule out calculation; reasoning about numbers to *understand* a problem is not antithetical to reasoning with numbers to *get* an answer (Keeley & Tobey, 2011).

Some properties of science and math are wide open for discovery and debate, while other things are known and settled. It is up to the instructor to help students recognize the difference while arousing natural curiosity and creative thinking.

SUMMARY AND CONCLUSION

A science or math lesson plan is a format for implementing the teacher's goals and objectives in a way that connects to the district curriculum and subject-matter standards. It should include methods of assessment that go beyond measuring outcomes to outlining how student learning can be improved as it is happening.

By developing lesson plans that support student learning and provide for purposeful feedback, teachers can take accountability into their own hands. Experienced teachers recognize the fact that there should be space for reasoning skills and the creative imagination in any plan.

Whether you call it formative, informative, or transformative assessment, student/teacher feedback, discussion, and observation during class activities provide useful information about learning while it is happening. The next step is quickly acting on that information in a way that improves student learning.

When done right, ongoing assessment activates students and encourages them to assume ownership of their own learning (McMillan, 2007). Along the way, students can learn to assess their own work using agreed-upon criteria for success.

In the differentiated classroom, the teacher also focuses on giving learners the opportunity to use their ideas and the information they gather to inquire about a topic and propose unique solutions to problems. In such a supportive learning community, time is set aside for personal reflection and engaging feedback from peers. It is also important to note that thinking and interaction do not stop when the inquiry is over or the problem has been solved.

Like the science standards, the math standards provide a useful vision and helpful guide for lesson planning as we look to the future. Both sets of standards recommend engaging students in authentic practices and meaningful learning experiences. Also, both suggest that various forms of formative and performance assessments can be powerful tools for guiding instruction, facilitating learning, and meeting the needs of individual learners.

Open questions and parallel tasks can help teachers reach across cultural boundaries. But teachers can't overcome all problems associated with a student's home environment. Although few want to talk about it, poverty and racial separation are the two biggest negative influences when it comes to school achievement (Ravitch, 2010).

Everyone has some direct or indirect responsibility when it comes to the education of children and young adults. But when it comes to school-based learning, what's most important for a student's academic success is having teachers who are enthusiastic about what they are teaching and know *the characteristics of effective instruction*.

When it comes to informed citizenship, we must all have some understanding of the role of science and math in our lives. Just as important, we all need to consider how products of both domains, like technology, will become ever more central to our lives in the future.

The best of today's approaches to science and mathematics instruction can serve as road maps to a bright future. If these subjects are taught well, it is possible that in tomorrow's schools, students will find them useful, interesting, and even beautiful. Science and math are, after all, two of the more likely places to find fresh ideas that can lead to unexpected answers. To paraphrase John Schaar: The future is not some place we are going to, but one we are creating, the paths to it are not found but made, and the activity of making them changes both the maker and the destination.

DISCUSSION POINTS FOR TEACHERS

1. How does equal access to quality science or math learning experiences encourage the development of informed participants in a democratic society?
2. Do you think that good resources can replace a science or math textbook for your students? How could you use rich resources *and* an up-to-date textbook? How might a teacher's edition to the textbook help you?
3. How would you check for student misperceptions *during* their work on a unit or on a lesson that lasts several days?
4. Collect five or six lesson plan formats from experienced teachers (or on the Internet) and look for common features. How might you combine elements of several and build in more room for differentiation and informative assessment?

REFERENCES

Burke, K. (2010). *Balanced assessment: From formative to summative.* Bloomington, IN: Solution Tree Press.
Chapman, C., & King, R. (2008). *Differentiated instructional management: Work smarter, not harder.* Thousand Oaks, CA: Corwin Press.
Domine, V. (2009). *Rethinking technology in schools.* New York, NY: Peter Lang Publishers.
Estrin, J. (2008). *Closing the innovation gap: Reigniting the spark of creativity in a global economy.* New York, NY: McGraw-Hill.
Gardner, H. (2006). *Five minds for the future.* Boston, MA: Harvard Business School Press.
Gareis, C., & Grant, L. (2008). *Teacher-made assessments: How to connect curriculum, instruction, and student learning.* Larchmont, NY: Eye On Education.
Gregory, G., & Hammerman, E. (2008). *Differentiated instructional strategies for science, grades K–8.* Thousand Oaks, CA: Corwin Press.
Hibbard, K. M. (2008). *Performance-based learning and assessment in middle school.* Larchmont, NY: Eye On Education.
Keeley, P. (2008). *Science formative assessment: 75 practical strategies for linking assessment, instruction, and learning.* Thousand Oaks, CA: Corwin Press.
Keeley, P., & Tobey, C. (2011). *Mathematics formative assessment: Practical strategies for linking assessment, instruction, and learning.* Thousand Oaks, CA: Corwin/NCTM.
McMillan, J. (Ed.). (2007). *Formative classroom practice: Theory into practice.* New York, NY: Teachers College Press.
Peterson, I. (1994). Catching the flutter of a falling leaf. *Science News, 146,* 183.
Popham, W. J. (2008) *Transformative assessment.* Alexandria, VA: Association for Supervision and Curriculum Development.
Ravitch, D. (2010). *The death and life of the great American school system: How testing and choice are undermining education.* New York, NY: Basic Books.
Sousa, D. (2008). *How the brain learns mathematics.* Thousand Oaks, CA: Corwin Press.
Stiggins, R., Chappuis, S., & Arter, J. (2012). *Classroom assessment for student learning: Doing it right—using it well.* Upper Saddle River, NJ: Pearson Education.
Tomlinson, C., Brimijoin, K., & Narvaez, L. (2008). *The differentiated school: Making revolutionary change in teaching and learning.* Alexandria, VA: Association for Supervision and Curriculum Development.

Tomlinson, C., & Cunningham-Edison, C. (2003). *Differentiation in practice: A resource guide for differentiating curriculum.* Alexandria, VA: Association for Supervision and Curriculum Development.

Wright, W. (2008). *Spore.* Electronic Arts. This is a simulation where players experience the evolution of life through billions of years. It doesn't perfectly mirror nature, but it is a good way to get middle-school students to think about the evolutionary process.

Zembal-Saul, C., McNeill, K., & Harshburger, K. (2012). *What's the evidence? Engaging K–5 students in constructing explanations in science.* Upper Saddle River, NJ: Pearson Education.

www.ingramcontent.com/pod-product-compliance
Lightning Source LLC
Chambersburg PA
CBHW052132300426
44116CB00010B/1871